BUDDHISM
WORLD RELIGIONS

by Madhu Bazaz Wangu

☑® Facts On File, Inc.

BUDDHISM, Revised Editon
World Religions

Copyright © 2002, 1993 by Madhu Bazaz Wangu

Facts On File, Inc.
132 West 31st Street
New York, NY 10001

Library of Congress Cataloging-in-Publication Data
Wangu, Madhu Bazaz.
Buddhism / Madhu Bazaz Wangu.– Rev. ed.
        p. cm. — (World religions)
Includes bibliographical references and index.
        ISBN 0-8160-4728-6
        1. Buddhism – Juvenile literature. 2. Buddhism. I. Title. II. Series.
BQ277.W36 2002
294.3—dc21   2002019997

You can find Facts On File on the World Wide Web at **http://www.factsonfile.com**

Developed by Brown Publishing Network, Inc.
Design Production by Jennifer Angell/Brown Publishing Network, Inc.
Photo Research by Nina Whitney
Photo credits:
Cover: Painting, Vairocana, Po Monastery in Spiti, Tibet. 12th century. ACSAA Slide Collection, University of Michigan. Title page: The Bettmann Archive. Table of Contents page: Photo courtesy of Korean Overseas Information Service. *Pages 6–7* The Bettmann Archive; *9* **Seated Buddha**, Chinese, T'ang Dynasty. Early 8th century. Gilt bronze, 8". Metropolitan Museum of Art, Rogers Fund, 1943; *11* Bruce Stromberg, ASIA IMAGES; *12* Photo courtesy of Korean Overseas Information Service; *14* Bonnie Kamin; *16–17* The Bettmann Archive; *23* UPI/Bettmann; *25* The Newark Museum; *30* UPI/Bettmann; *32–33* The Bettmann Archive; *35* The Bettmann Archive; *37* Wide World; *38* AP/Wide World; *47* Sekai Bunka Photo, Shashinka Photo Library; *50–51* Sekai Bunka Photo, Shashinka Photo Library; *52* Art Resource; *55* **Guanyin.** Wood with polychrome and gilt. 11th century, Chinese. The Saint Louis Art Museum; *59* UPI/Bettmann; *68–69* UPI/Bettmann; *82–83* Photo courtesy of Korean Overseas Information Service; *87* AP/Wide World; *90* Sekai Bunka Photo, Shashinka Photo Library; *93* Carmel Berkson photo from Art Resource; *98–99* AP/Wide World; *104* Courtesy Ceylon Tourist Board; *105* Bonnie Kamin; *107* Courtesy Ceylon Tourist Board; *110–111* UPI/Bettmann; *112* UPI/Bettmann; *116* Religious News Service; *121* AP/Wide World; *122* AP/Wide World

Printed in the United States of America
RRD PKG 10 9 8 7 6 5 4 3 2
This book is printed on acid-free paper.

TABLE OF CONTENTS

Preface

We live in what is sometimes described as a "secular age," meaning, in effect, that religion is not an especially important issue for most people. But there is much evidence to suggest that this is not true. In many societies, including the United States, religion and religious values shape the lives of millions of individuals and play a key role in politics and culture as well.

The World Religions series, of which this book is a part, is designed to appeal to both students and general readers. The books offer clear, accessible overviews of the major religious traditions and institutions of our time. Each volume in the series describes where a particular religion is practiced, its origins and history, its central beliefs and important rituals, and its contributions to world civilization. Carefully chosen photographs complement the text, and a glossary and bibliography are included to help readers gain a more complete understanding of the subject at hand.

Religious institutions and spirituality have always played a central role in world history. These books will help clarify what religion is all about and reveal both the similarities and differences in the great spiritual traditions practiced around the world today.

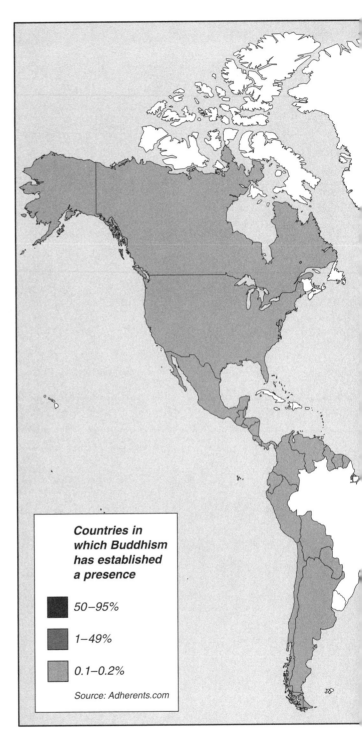

Countries in which Buddhism has established a presence

- 50–95%
- 1–49%
- 0.1–0.2%

Source: Adherents.com

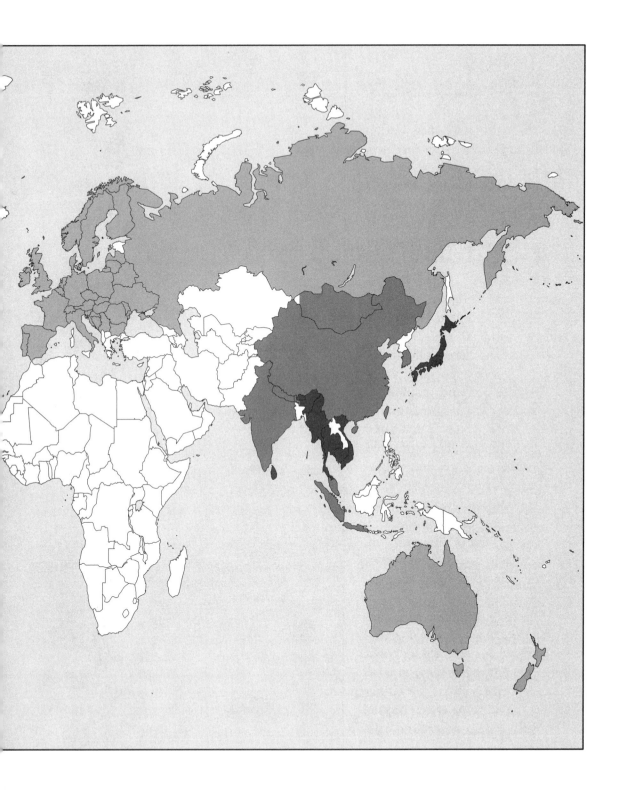

CHAPTER 1

Introduction: The Modern Buddhist World

*A*pproximately 350 million people in the world today are practicing Buddhists, making Buddhism the fourth largest of the world's religions. However Buddhism has an influence even greater than the number of its adherents would indicate. From the time that *Siddhartha Gautama*—known as *the Buddha*—first preached his simple doctrine about 2500 years ago, Buddhism has spread throughout Asia from its homeland in India. It has had a significant and lasting impact on India, China, Japan, Korea, Thailand, Tibet and other Asian nations.

Today, Buddhism is the majority religion in Japan, Tibet, Laos, Myanmar (formerly Burma), Singapore, Sri Lanka, Taiwan, Thailand, Cambodia, Bhutan, and Vietnam. Though the most populous nation in the world, China, is officially atheist, a sizable minority of its people adhere to Buddhist beliefs. Millions more Chinese, though they are not practicing Buddhists, are influenced by the cultural aspects of Buddhism.

Buddhism is not confined solely to Asia. In the past century, it has won admirers and followers in Europe and the United States. Indeed, the majority of the people in one of the states of the United States, Hawaii, are Buddhists.

All the countries that came under the influence of Buddhism were enriched culturally and artistically. The image of the Buddha appears in colossal statues, delicate figurines, and innumerable styles of art throughout Asia. Scenes from the Buddha's life are as important in Asian art as the story of Jesus Christ is in Western art.

What Is Buddhism?

Buddhism is a path to spiritual discovery. Its founder, Siddhartha Gautama, looked at the human condition, much as a doctor does. He found disease, decay, and death. He fully realized that joy and pleasure existed as well, but he recognized that those qualities did not last. All things in life were transient or temporary. So even in joy, the awareness of impermanence and death caused suffering.

Because of his Indian background, Siddhartha did not believe that death was a final release from suffering. For in Indian religious tradition, after death souls are reborn into new bodies. The cycle of birth, death, and rebirth goes on unendingly. All living beings were caught in this cycle. Siddhartha strove to find a way to get off the treadmill of endless rebirths.

Siddhartha devoted his life to pondering this problem. He practiced severe self-denial and meditation until he reached an answer. In the moment of his insight he became the Buddha, a title that means "the enlightened" or "the awakened."

The Buddha diagnosed human desire in all its forms as the cause of suffering. Therefore, his "treatment," or solution, was to eliminate desire by "right thoughts and right actions." This could be done by following the Eightfold Path. This was a series of eight stages of a high ethical code. The first stages on this path were guides, calling for kindly behavior to all living things. Later stages were more difficult and required meditation and long discipline.

This truth, or law, of Buddhism is known as *Dharma*. Indeed, Buddhadharma is the name of the religion in Asia. It is also called "the Middle Way." The Buddha advised those who wished to follow the Dharma to avoid extremes of behavior, such as severe self-denial or, at the other extreme, selfish attachment to pleasure. He stated, "Avoid these two extremes: attachment to the

pleasures of the senses, which is low and vulgar, and attachment to self-mortification, which is painful. Both are unprofitable."

During his lifetime, the Buddha institutionalized his teachings by forming *Sangha*. The Sangha is the community of monks and nuns who practice the religion and teach it to others. Today the members of the Sangha provide a living link with their religion's founder.

Correctly following the Eightfold Path brings one, in time, to *Nirvana*, a term that is difficult to define. Buddhists have said that it cannot be described in words. It is not the heaven of Christianity or Islam. In Sanskrit, the ancient Indian language, Nirvana means "blowing out" (as a flame is blown out). What is blown out is hatred, greed, and delusion.

Looking at it in another way, Nirvana is the loss of the "ego" or "I" self, a condition that ends the path of suffering and pain when human beings travel from one life to another. The word Nirvana also implies "boundless expansion," which may be described as becoming part of the universe. It was Nirvana that Siddhartha attained when he became the Buddha.

Buddhism is like other religions in its concern for the welfare of humankind—indeed, for all living things. In the striving for the attainment of Nirvana, it teaches a high ethical code. It asks its followers to abstain from taking life of any kind; to not lie, cheat or steal; and to treat others with kindness. "Hatred does not cease by hatred at any time," said the Buddha. "Hatred ceases by love."

Yet in significant ways, Buddhism is different from other major religions. It has no description of a Supreme Being, for the Buddha was an agnostic. Buddhism has no single creed that its adherents must believe. It demands no exclusive allegiance from its followers, as the monotheistic religions do. There is no counterpart to the Judeo-Christian commandment, "Thou shalt have no other gods before me." Nor are there ceremonies or rites that a Buddhist must follow (though many have been developed by the different branches of the religion). Buddhism's appeal has rested solely on the message of its founder and its flexibility in adapting to different cultures and philosophies.

The Great Variety of Buddhism

Like Christ and Muhammad, the founders of Christianity and Islam, the Buddha never wrote down his teachings. His disciples memorized his words, and their followers carried on the oral tradition. The first comprehensive written record of the Buddha's doctrine was not compiled until 500 years after his death.

■ *For hate is not conquered by hate: hate is conquered by love. This is a law eternal.*
From the **Dhammapada** (1:5)

■ *Only a man himself can be the master of himself: who else from outside could be his master? When the Master and servant are one, then there is true help and self possession.*
From the **Dhammapada** (12:160)

By that time, Buddhism had already developed two major forms: *Theravada Buddhism* and *Mahayana Buddhism*. In general, Theravada's adherents followed more literally the teachings of the historic Buddha, while the followers of Mahayana more freely adapted the Buddha's doctrine.

By and large, Theravada Buddhism is followed today by people on the southern rim of Asia—Sri Lanka, Myanmar, Thailand, Cambodia, Laos, and parts of Malaysia. Mahayana Buddhism spread north and east from India—into China, Tibet, Vietnam, Korea, and Japan.

■ *The front view of the Buddhist temple of Wat Phra Keo, Bangkok, Thailand*

Buddhism was never spread by conquering armies or by forced conversions of unbelievers. In fact, over the centuries, Mahayana Buddhism has coexisted easily with other religions and traditions. This attitude is strikingly different from the monotheistic religions of the West, but is entirely consistent with the Asian approach to religion. In Asia, one truth does not have to supplant or drive out another. Buddhism offered one path to salvation that people could follow without abandoning their own traditions. Often Buddhism adopted and adapted new forms and customs from existing religions.

■ *Buddhists celebrate the Buddha's Birth, Enlightenment and Parinirvana (the final passing away) on the same day of the year, called Wesak or Vaishakha. Lighted candles are one of the most important ritual ingredients. While the lighted wick symbolizes wisdom, melting wax symbolizes compassion and the impermanence of existence.*

In China, for example, Buddhism became one of "the Three Great Truths." The other two were Confucianism and Taoism. For centuries, the Chinese people followed all three of these "truths," and saw no contradiction in doing so.

Missionaries from China spread Buddhism to Korea, and from there it came to Japan. The Japanese, showing their ingenious talent for turning foreign things into uniquely Japanese traditions, assimilated Buddhism into their culture. Most Japanese today follow the practices of both Buddhism and Shinto, the ancient Japanese belief in kami, or nature-spirits.

As a result of its tolerant tradition, Buddhism today displays a wide variety of practices and customs. In Thailand, during the rainy season that begins in July, school children make candles to donate to the local Buddhist temple, and celebrate with song and dance. Each year in Sri Lanka, orange-robed Buddhist monks lead an elephant through the streets. It carries one of the country's holiest Buddhist relics—a tooth of the Buddha himself. In Tibet, spiritual guides called *lamas* gather around people who are dying, reciting certain texts to assist the dying person to reach a higher plane of existence. In Korea, each April, shops and houses are festooned with paper lanterns as colorful processions pass through the streets in celebration of the Buddha's birthday. In Japan, many people simply recite the phrase "I call on the Amida Buddha" in their everyday lives. All these people are paying homage to the Buddha.

The message of Buddhism has an appeal on many different intellectual levels. It can be either very simple or immensely complicated. For the person with such everyday concerns as how to earn a living, it offers a moral message of compassion, honesty, and self-control. Its appeal is as great to a practitioner in industrial Japan as it is to peasants in rural communities of Southeast Asia. On the other hand, it can provide a basis for lifelong meditation and thought.

Today, members of the Sangha still teach and pursue the goal of *enlightenment*. Men and women put on the robes of Buddhist monks or nuns and enter monasteries. They spend much of their time reciting together the scriptures of Buddhism, or in solitary meditation on the truths of the religion. They depend on

> ■ As the bee takes the essence of a flower and flies away without destroying its beauty and perfume, so let the sage (holy person) wander in this life.
> From the **Dhammapada** (4:49)

■ *Two Buddhist monks on an alms round in Chiangmai, Thailand. Note the interesting juxtaposition of Pepsi advertisement and monks.*

the donations of the faithful for their existence. Some take their begging-bowls into the streets, and others receive donations of food or money at the monastery.

Like Buddhism itself, the life of a monk or nun is flexible. Some people enter as children and stay for their entire lifetimes. Others lead the monastic life for a short time and then return to the everyday world. This is not frowned upon, for they have earned merit for the time they spent in complete devotion to the

Buddhist way. In the countries of Southeast Asia, it is very common for the lay people—like successful merchants and craftspeople—to enter a monastery for the months of the rainy season, and then go back to their work.

Amid all the different forms and practices of the religion, one of the few things all agree on is that a Buddhist "takes refuge" in the Three Jewels. These are the Buddha, the Dharma, and the Sangha. Indeed, many Buddhists recite the phrase "I take refuge in the Buddha, I take refuge in the Dharma, and I take refuge in the Sangha," as a daily prayer. When Buddhists speak of taking refuge, they mean following the path that leads to the end of suffering—Nirvana. A Tibetan proverb sums up the Three Jewels: "The Buddha is the great physician; the Dharma is the remedy; the Sangha is the nurse who administers the remedy."

The Universal Appeal of Buddhism

Buddhism has a universal appeal. It recognizes the suffering that all people endure, and provides a way to overcome it. Anyone can practice it, for as the Buddha said, "My doctrine makes no distinction between high and low, rich and poor; it is like the sky, it has room for all; like water it washes all alike."

Though its roots are in Asia, as a living faith, Buddhism continues to attract followers in all parts of the world. In Great Britain alone, the number of Buddhist centers has grown from about a half dozen in the 1950s to several hundred today. Buddhism is also becoming popular in the countries of the former Soviet Union, including Russia.

The Buddha's Dharma has stood the test of time. It is practical, for it provides specific action and stresses individual effort. The Buddha said that he himself could only point the way. Each person must follow the Eightfold Path on his or her own. "Look within yourself," he told his followers, "thou art the Buddha."

CHAPTER 2

The Life of
the Buddha

*P*rince Siddhartha Gautama, who would become known as the Buddha, was born around the year 563 B.C.E. His birthplace was the town of Kapilavastu in what is now Nepal. Siddhartha was the son of Shuddhodana, the chief (sometimes called a rajah, or king) of the Sakyas. Hence the title Sakyamuni, or "Sage of the Sakyas," by which Siddhartha was later known.

There is no doubt that Siddhartha really existed. About 250 years after his death, an Indian emperor set up inscribed stone pillars at the important sites of Siddhartha's life and teachings. These are regarded as reliable historical records.

Moreover, the details of the Buddha's life, as retold in this chapter, come from an oral tradition begun by those who actually knew and saw him. These accounts were not written down until around 500 years after his death. They contain many miraculous elements, which Buddhists accept as historical truth. Students of religious history may regard them in the same way as Christ's miracles and resurrection, Moses' reception of the commandments from God, or the archangel Gabriel's revelations to the prophet Muhammad.

According to the Buddhist tradition, Siddhartha's mother, Queen Maya, was a woman "of perfect form and bee-black tresses, fearless in heart and full of grace and virtue." One day, a feeling of great peace and joy came over her. That night, while she slept, she had a wonderful dream: An elephant with six tusks, carrying a lotus flower in its trunk, touched her right side. At that moment, her son was miraculously conceived.

■ Queen Maya's
(Buddha's mother) dream

When the queen told her husband of the dream, he called Brahmins, or learned men, to interpret it. They predicted that the child would be either the greatest king in the world or the greatest ascetic, a holy man who practices self-denial. His name would be Siddhartha, which means "he whose aim is accomplished."

Accompanied by dancing women and guards, Queen Maya went to her father's home to prepare for the birth. As she stepped from her chariot in the Lumbini Gardens, she stopped to rest, taking hold of a branch of a sal tree.

Legend tells us that at that moment, Buddha emerged from her right side. Without any help, the infant walked seven steps in each of the four directions of the compass. In his footprints, lotus flowers sprouted from the earth. The miraculous infant announced, "No further births have I to endure, for this is my last body. Now shall I destroy and pluck out by the roots the sorrow that is caused by birth and death.

Seven days after the wondrous birth, Queen Maya died. Hence Mahaprajapati, Maya's sister, looked after Siddhartha.

The Great Renunciation

The prediction of the learned men had disturbed Siddhartha's father, King Shuddhodana. From the time of his son's birth, Shuddhodana encouraged his son to follow the path of kingship. Shuddhodana surrounded his son with pleasures and granted his every wish. Never did Siddhartha see or learn about any kind of suffering or hardship. When he left the palace, the king's guards went ahead of his chariot, clearing the streets of anything unpleasant or disturbing.

A Brahmin priest instructed Siddhartha in the ways of government, preparing him to govern wisely. Siddhartha also learned the arts of war—how to fight with a sword and shoot an arrow from his bow. The young man was strong and healthy, and his physical beauty and lively spirit attracted many friends. All of his companions were children of the officials of the court.

When Siddhartha was about twenty, he married Yasodhara, the daughter of one of the king's ministers. Their wedding feast lasted for many days, and gifts were distributed to the people of the kingdom to mark the occasion. Within a year, Yasodhara bore Siddhartha's son, named Rahula, which means "fetter" or "impediment."

King Shuddodana was pleased, for he had provided everything his son would need for happiness in his life and success as a great king. Some years passed, during which time Siddhartha lived in the palace with his wife and son, enjoying all the pleasures of a king.

Then, when he was twenty-nine years old, Siddhartha asked his charioteer, Channa, to take him for a ride without the consent of the king. As the prince rode through the city, he saw three things that he had never seen before. One was an old man, one was a man suffering from illness, and the third was a corpse surrounded by mourners.

Siddhartha asked Channa to explain the meaning of these strange sights. Channa responded that old age, sickness, and death were natural and unavoidable things that came to all people. They were to be endured.

Shocked, Siddhartha returned to the palace and thought about what he had seen. For the first time, he confronted the reality of life: "Everything is transient; nothing is permanent in this world....Knowing that, I can find delight in nothing....How can a man, who knows that death is quite inevitable, still feel greed in his heart, enjoy the world of senses and not weep in this great danger?"

Once more, Siddhartha asked Channa to take him into the city. This time, he saw the last of the "Four Sights" that changed his life. This was a wandering holy man, an ascetic, with no possessions. The man had shaved his head, wore only a ragged yellow robe, and carried a walking-staff. Siddhartha stopped his chariot and questioned the man. The ascetic told the prince, "I am...terrified by birth and death and therefore have adopted a homeless life to win salvation....I search for the most blessed state in which suffering, old age, and death are unknown."

That very night, Siddhartha resolved to renounce the life of pleasure in the palace. He silently kissed his sleeping wife and young son and ordered Channa to drive him out of the city. Legend claims that celestial beings held up the hooves of the horses so that their clatter would not wake the guards. At the edge of a forest, Siddhartha took off his jeweled sword, cut off his hair and beard, and discarded his princely garments. He put on the yellow robe of a holy man, and told Channa to take his possessions back to his father.

The Great Retirement

Siddhartha wandered through northeastern India, seeking out holy men, who taught him ancient Indian techniques of meditation. But his main quest was to find the answer to the problem of suffering. He wanted to know why people suffered, and how this suffering could end.

Siddhartha studied the teachings of Hinduism, the ancient religion of India. He was most influenced by the concept of *Samsara*. Samsara is a belief that after death, a person's innermost essence, or soul, transmigrates into a new body—it is born again. Another name for this process is reincarnation.

When a soul is reborn, it may enter a body in a higher or lower state of existence than its previous one. The new body may be that of a king, a beggar, or even an animal or insect. The determining factor of a soul's new existence is the quality of life led by the individual soul in its previous existence. This is called the law of *Karma*. Simply put, Karma consists of the individual's thoughts, words, and deeds in his or her previous existences. If the Karma has been good, the soul will be reborn in a higher form. Conversely, if the Karma has been bad, the soul is punished (pays a "Karmic price") by being reborn in a lower form. Human suffering, therefore, was the result of some bad Karma that a person had accumulated in a previous lifetime.

The law of Karma also had social implications. Indian society was strictly divided into four castes, or classes. At the top were the Brahmins—priests and religious teachers. The second caste included the warriors and rulers. It was within this caste that Siddhartha was born. The third and fourth castes were the merchants and workers (labourers, craftsmen, farmers and so on). At the very bottom were people who were literally out-castes, below the four castes, whose station in life made them impure.

In a single lifetime, it was impossible to rise within the caste system. By law and tradition, the members of each caste were strictly separated from the others. People of different castes did not marry, eat together, or have physical contact with one another. If a person violated the caste rules, he or she had to undergo rituals of purification. The only way to move up was to accumulate good Karma and be reborn into a higher caste.

Some Hindus believed that Samsara—this process of life, death, and rebirth—was an endless chain of existence. It would continue forever, from life to life. Around the time of Siddhartha's life, however, new teachings—later set down in scriptures called the Upanishads—were being developed. The Upanishadic teachers developed the idea of *Moksha*, or release. By leading a highly spiritual life (or several lives), a soul could be reunited with Brahman, the Ultimate Reality. The cycle of Samsara would be broken.

Attracted by this idea, Siddhartha adopted a life of extreme self-denial and penances, meditating constantly. He settled on the bank of the Nairanjana River, determined to force himself into the state of mind that would lead to moksha. For six years, through rain and wind, hot and cold weather, he stayed there, eating and drinking only enough to stay alive. His body became emaciated, and his former physical strength left him. His holiness was so evident that five other holy men joined him, hoping to learn from his example.

■ *Fasting Siddhartha—in search of Enlightenment*

The Enlightenment

One day, the Buddhist tradition holds, Siddhartha realized that his years of penance had only weakened his body. In such a state of physical exhaustion, he could not meditate properly. He stood up and stepped into the river to bathe. But he was so weak that he could not raise himself out of the water. The Buddhist

■ *The shrine of Bodh Gaya, India. The tree stands where it is believed the original Bodhi tree (under which the Buddha attained enlightenment) grew.*

scriptures say that the trees on the river bank bent their branches down so that he could reach them.

At that moment, a milk-maid named Nandabala came into sight. She offered Siddhartha a bowl of milk and rice, and he accepted it gratefully. When the five holy men who had been his pupils saw this, they left because they thought he had abandoned his quest to achieve true holiness or moksha.

Refreshed by the meal, Siddhartha sat down under a fig tree (known to Buddhists as the *Bo tree*, the Tree of Enlightenment) and resolved that he would not arise until he had found the answer he had sought for so long.

The Buddhist scriptures say that Mara, an evil god who constantly tempted people with desire, saw that Siddhartha was near to his goal. Mara sent his three sons and three daughters to tempt Siddhartha. They tormented him with thirst, lust, and discontent, offering all sorts of pleasures to distract him.

But Siddhartha was not swayed by them. He entered a state of deep meditation, in which he recalled all his previous rebirths. He gained knowledge of the cycle of births and deaths, and the certainty that he had cast off the ignorance and passion of the "I" self that bound him to the world. At last, he had attained enlightenment.

This experience was the beginning of the history of Buddhism as a religion. Siddhartha became the Buddha, the "enlightened one." His own desire and suffering were over and, as the Buddha, he experienced Nirvana. In the Buddha's words, "There is a sphere which is neither earth, nor water, nor fire, nor air...which is neither this world nor the other world, neither sun nor moon. I deny that it is coming or going, enduring, death or birth. It is only the end of suffering."

As tradition has it, the Buddha could then have cast off his body and his existence. Instead, however, he made a great act of self-sacrifice. Having discovered the way to end his own suffering, he turned back, determined to share his enlightenment with others so that all living souls could end the cycles of their own rebirth and suffering. He thus set an example of compassion and wisdom or self-knowledge for others that would be a hallmark of his followers.

Setting in Motion the Wheel of Doctrine

Buddha went to the city of Sarnath, where he found the five ascetics who had deserted him earlier. They were sitting in a deer park. Seeing him approach, they decided not to greet him by the respectful title they had used to address him before. But when he appeared before them, they saw signs on his body and head that indicated he had risen to a higher state of holiness.

The Buddha began to teach them what he had discovered. He took a handful of rice grains and drew a wheel on the ground. This represented the wheel of life that went on for existence after

■ *An early-nineteenth-century Tibetan painting depicts the Wheel of Existence, which exhibits the causes of suffering and the stages of endless becomings.*

existence. (The symbol of the wheel is often used to stand for Buddhist teaching.) This preaching was called his Deer Park Sermon, or "Setting in Motion the Wheel of Doctrine."

Siddhartha Gautama revealed that he had become the Buddha. He described the life of pleasure that he had first known, and then the life of severe asceticism that he had practiced. Neither of these was the true path to Nirvana. Instead, the Buddha advised the Middle Way, which keeps aloof from both extremes. "To satisfy the necessities of life is not evil," the Buddha said. "To keep the body in good health is a duty, for otherwise we shall not be able to trim the lamp of wisdom, and keep our mind strong and clear."

The Buddha explained the Four Noble Truths and the Eightfold Path that were the heart of his teaching. The Four Noble Truths were the Buddha's analysis of the cause of suffering. The Eightfold Path was the solution. Together they formed the Dharma, or the doctrine of Buddhism.

The Four Noble Truths are:

1. Suffering consists of disease, old age, and death; of separation from those we love; of craving what we cannot obtain; and of hating what we cannot avoid.
2. All suffering is caused by desire and the attempt to satisfy our desires.
3. Therefore, suffering can be overcome by ceasing to desire.
4. The way to end desire is to follow the Eightfold Path.

The Eightfold Path is a series of eight stages that leads to the end of desire. The first of these are attainable in everyday life; the later ones require more effort and concentration. Like many of Buddha's teachings, they appear simple at first, but take on subtle and intricate meaning when studied closely.

The Eightfold Path is:

1. Right opinion
2. Right intentions
3. Right speech
4. Right conduct
5. Right livelihood
6. Right effort
7. Right mindfulness
8. Right concentration

The first of these, right opinion, concerns understanding the Four Truths. Then, through right intentions, a person decides to set his or her life on the correct path. Right speech consists of not lying, not criticizing others unjustly, not using harsh language or gossiping. Right conduct means to abstain from killing, stealing, cruelty, or lustful activities. To follow right livelihood a person must earn a living in a way that does not harm any living thing. To practice right effort, a person must conquer all evil thoughts, and strive to arouse and maintain only good thoughts. Right mindfulness has a special meaning in Buddhism, in which a person becomes intensely aware of all the states of his or her body, feeling, and mind. That leads to the final stage, right concentration, which is deep meditation that leads to a higher stage of consciousness. A person who practices right concentration will come to the enlightenment that Siddhartha attained.

The five ascetics immediately recognized that the Buddha had found the correct way. They became his first disciples. For the next forty-five years, he traveled through northeastern India, preaching the Dharma and answering the questions of those who wished to learn it.

In his teachings, the Buddha retained many elements of the Hinduism of his time, including the concepts of Samsara and Karma. However, the Buddhist Dharma differed from Hinduism in certain important respects.

The Buddha challenged the authority of the Brahmins, the highest caste in Hindu society. He opposed the animal sacrifices that only Brahmin priests could perform. Hinduism made extensive use of animal sacrifices to its various gods. In contrast, the Buddha told his followers not to kill any living creature. In addition, the Buddha did not accept the Brahmins' special role as interpreters of religious truth. Instead, the Buddha stressed that anyone, regardless of caste, who followed the Eightfold Path could achieve Nirvana.

The Buddha also questioned the Hindu idea of the *Atman*, or soul—the individual consciousness that was reborn again and again. He denied there was any personal, eternal soul or permanent self. Instead, the Buddha compared the individual to a cart. A cart was made up of different elements—wheels, body, yoke. Separately, they were not a cart. Only when they were together did they form a cart. In the same way, Buddha taught, an individual is composed of five elements called *Skandhas*, which were constantly in a state of change. The Skandhas were: form and matter, sensations, ideas, emotions, and consciousness. What was

■ *Health is the greatest possession. Contentment is the greatest treasure. Confidence is the greatest friend. Nirvana is the greatest joy.*
From the **Dhammapada** *(15:204)*

reborn over and over were groups of ever-changing Skandhas, influenced by Karma. Thus, the Skandhas reborn were not exactly the same as the Skandhas that had died.

The Buddha declared that by following his Eightfold Path, people would lose their false idea of self, and achieve Nirvana. When a person reached Nirvana, the "cart" would dissolve. After that, a person would no longer accumulate bad Karma even if his life continued.

As for Brahman itself—a Hindu concept we might liken to a Supreme Being—Buddha refused to consider whether or not such a universal soul existed. Once, when a Hindu scholar pressed the Buddha to debate the existence of Brahman, he replied that the scholar was like a man who finds himself in a burning house. The scholar wanted to find out who set the fire or how it started, when he should be thinking first of getting out of the house. The Hindu goal of Moksha—or union of the soul with Brahman—was replaced, in Buddhism, by the goal of achieving Nirvana.

The simplicity of the Buddha's teaching, its emphasis on personal action, and the Buddha's opposition to the caste system, soon won him many followers. Like other religious teachers, Buddha often used stories or parables to explain his doctrine. In the Parable of the Mustard Seed, the Buddha taught the lesson of facing and accepting suffering.

Once a distraught woman brought the body of her dead son to the Buddha. She begged him to bring the boy back to life. The Buddha asked the woman to bring him a tiny mustard seed. But he made one condition: the seed must be one that came from a house in which no death had ever occurred. The woman searched but could not find such a house. Instead, she saw people who had suffered losses like her own. In her search, her own pain lessened as compassion for the pain of others increased. The Buddha wanted her to realize that death was normal and universal. Only through facing the human situation "as it really is" could she start her own journey on the Eightfold Path.

Beginning with the five disciples he spoke to in the Deer Park, certain people embraced the Buddha's teachings so completely that they accompanied him everywhere. He set rules of conduct for them, thus organizing the Sangha, which became a community of monks (later, nuns as well). The members of the Sangha are known as *bhikkus*. The Sangha served two functions. First, the monks were charged with preserving and teaching the Dharma. Second, the Sangha enabled bhikkus to concentrate on the goal of Nirvana. Only people who spent time in meditation could achieve the last two steps of the Eightfold Path.

The Buddha made another break with Hindu tradition when he permitted women to join the Sangha. The first Buddhist nun was the Buddha's aunt, who had raised him.

These Buddhist monks and nuns followed the Buddha's example of wandering from place to place, spreading his teaching. They were allowed to possess only a beggar's bowl, a razor, a needle, a strainer, a staff, a toothpick, and a robe. (The strainer was to remove insects that had fallen into their drink, so they would not be consumed and killed.)

During India's long, hot, rainy season, the members of the Sangha settled in *Viharas*, or resting places. These were the beginnings of the great monasteries that are today found in many parts of Asia.

The Buddha recognized that not everyone could give up his or her everyday life to become part of the Sangha. He also accepted the laity—followers *(upasaka)* who believed his teachings but did not follow the strict rule of the Sangha. People in everyday life could achieve merit by practicing good works and build good Karma. In a future rebirth they would be able to seek Nirvana. The Buddha encouraged the laity to follow as perfect a life as they could. As a guide to everyday behavior, the Buddha prescribed Five Precepts, or rules:

1. To refrain from taking life
2. To refrain from taking what is not given
3. To refrain from sexual misconduct
4. To refrain from false speech
5. To refrain from intoxicating things that cloud the mind

The Parinirvana

During the Buddha's travels, he returned to his birthplace in Kapilavastu. His father, Shuddhodana, was mortified to see his son begging for food. "No one in our family," said the king, "has

■ *A Buddhist priest is dwarfed by a twenty-six-foot-high statue of Ananda, Buddha's cousin and one of his major disciples. This statue stands next to the "Reclining Buddha." (See pages 110 and 111 of this book.)*

ever lived by begging." But the Buddha kissed his father's foot and said, "You belong to a noble line of kings. But I belong to the lineage of buddhas, and thousands of those have lived on alms."

Shuddhodana remembered the prophecy at Siddhartha's conception and became reconciled with his son. The Buddha's wife Yasodhara and son Rahula both joined the Sangha, as did his cousin Ananda, who became the Buddha's most faithful attendant during the later years of his life.

When Buddha was about eighty, a blacksmith named Cuanda gave him a meal that caused him to become ill. Buddha forced himself to walk on to the village of Kushinagara, where at last he lay down to rest in a grove of shala trees. As a crowd of followers gathered around him, he lay on his right side. Though it was not the season for blooming, the trees sprouted blossoms and showered them upon him. The scene has often been the inspiration for Buddhist artists.

Buddha told Ananda, "I am old and my journey is near its end. My body is like a worn-out cart held together only by the help of leather straps." Three times he asked the people gathered around him if they had any more questions about his teaching. Everyone remained silent.

The Buddha spoke his final words: "Everything that has been created is subject to decay and death. Everything is transitory. Work out your own salvation with diligence."

After passing through several states of meditation, the Buddha died—or, as Buddhists say, he reached his *Parinirvana*, "the cessation of perception and sensation."

During his long lifetime, the Buddha never traveled farther than 250 miles from Sarnath, the city where his teaching ministry began. However, he had set in motion a religious movement that would spread throughout the world and still remains a vital force 2500 years after his death.

CHAPTER 3

The Spread of Buddhism

*T*he Buddha urged his followers, "Go forth for the gain of the many, for the welfare of many, in compassion for the world. Preach the glorious doctrine; proclaim the life of holiness." By the time of his death, more than 500 monks lived in monasteries in the area where the Buddha had preached. Today, this region forms the Indian state of Bihar, whose name means "Buddhist monastery." From here, Buddhism began to spread westward through northern India.

About 200 years after the death of the Buddha, political developments encouraged the spread of the Dharma. Chandragupta Maurya conquered much of northern India, and created a strong, centralized empire. When Chandragupta's grandson, *Asoka*, became emperor around 270 B.C.E, the stage was set for Buddhism to move beyond the boundaries of India. The story of King Asoka's conversion is central to the historical progress of Buddhism.

Asoka

Asoka was an ambitious man. Through conquest, he expanded the *Maurya Empire,* absorbing central India as well as parts of many of the countries on modern India's northern border. He waged his fiercest campaign against the Kalingas, who lived in today's Orissa, in east central India. The struggle was so bloody that more than 100,000 Kalingas were slaughtered.

The carnage brought about a spiritual transformation in Asoka. He became a follower of Buddhism, and set up a stone pillar expressing remorse for his deeds: "After the conquest of Kalinga, the Beloved of the Gods (Asoka) began to follow Righteousness (Dharma), to love Righteousness, and to give instruction in Righteousness. Now the Beloved of the Gods regrets the conquest of Kalinga, for when an independent country is conquered people are killed, they die or are deported, and that the Beloved of the Gods finds very painful and grievous."

Asoka's conversion was no empty gesture, and thereafter he carried out policies designed to benefit his subjects. Along the roads throughout his empire, he ordered shelters built for travelers and banyan trees planted to provide shade for the footsore and weary. Asoka banned animal sacrifices and became a vegetarian himself. He abolished many cruel punishments for criminals. Hospitals were founded to serve both animals and humans. His government undertook the financial support of Buddhist monasteries. Asoka's actions made him the model Buddhist ruler. Later Buddhist kings throughout Asia would emulate his example.

As a permanent record of his reign, Asoka erected pillars throughout his empire. Inscribed in the language of its people, a form of Pali language, they proclaimed his achievements and ideals. Among these ideas was tolerance of all religions.

On a pillar that still stands in Delhi, Asoka ordered his philosophy inscribed in stone: "In religion is the chief excellence. Religion consists in good works, mercy, charity, purity and chastity. It consists in benevolence to the poor and to the afflicted, kindness to animals, to birds and to all creatures. Let all pay attention to this edict and let it endure for ages to come. He who acts in conformity with it shall attain to eternal happiness." This indeed is a noble statement of the ethics of Buddhism.

Wishing to carry the wisdom of the Buddha to the world, Asoka sent out missionaries in all directions. This historical event began the spread of the religion beyond its homeland. Some of Asoka's missionaries went as far west as Syria, Egypt, and the Greek world; others traveled south and north. Asoka began the process of making Buddhism a religion that would have followers throughout Asia.

■ Exquisitely carved with Buddhist symbols and Jataka stories, this eighteen-foot-high gateway to the largest dome-stupa in the world is in Sanchi, India. The stupa is believed to have been originally constructed by King Ashoka.

Buddhism spread along two major routes—one to the north across the land mass of Asia, and the other to the south across land and sea to southeastern Asia. Its expansion was always carried out peacefully. Never was it spread by soldiers or forced upon others by zealots of the faith. The message of Buddhism provided the appeal that attracted converts.

Sri Lanka

By tradition, Asoka's son Mahinda was a bhikku, or monk. His father entrusted him with carrying the Dharma to Ceylon. Today called Sri Lanka, Ceylon is a beautiful island off the tip of southern India. When Mahinda arrived, he was courteously received by the king, Tissa, at his capital at Anuradhapura. The king was impressed by the Buddhist teachings and converted in 247 B.C.E. Enthusiastic crowds gathered to hear Mahinda preach the Dharma. Soothsayers predicted, "These bhikkus will be lords upon this island."

King Tissa invited other Buddhist missionaries and donated a park for a Vihara. This monastery, the Mahavihara, became the center of Buddhism on the island. In his enthusiasm, King Tissa asked Mahinda whether the devotion showed by his people meant that Buddhism had struck deep roots in his country. Mahinda answered, "Not yet, Your Majesty. It has certainly sprung roots but they have not yet grown deep into the soil. Only when a sima (a monastery with the authority to ordain new monks) has been established and when a son born in Sri Lanka of Sri Lankan parents becomes a monk in Sri Lanka, only then will it be true to say that the roots of the Dharma are deeply embedded here." Within a short time these conditions were met.

Mahinda's sister, Sanghamitta, a Buddhist nun, soon followed her brother to Sri Lanka. Buddhist tradition says that before she left India, she picked a slip of the sacred Bo tree under which Siddartha Gautama had reached enlightenment. This was planted at a monastery in Anuradhapura. Today an enormous tree on this site is claimed to be the same one. Later saplings from this tree were planted throughout the island, providing a linkage through nature with the origins of Buddhism. Over time, Sri Lanka received other precious relics of the Buddha. These

■ *Peddlers in Sri Lanka carry decorative paper replicas of the Bodhi tree for the monthly Full Moon festival.*

included the Buddha's begging bowl, his tooth, and a collarbone. The introduction of Buddhism also brought writing, architecture, and sculpture to the island.

From the beginning, Buddhism was incorporated as the state religion of Sri Lanka. The Sri Lankan kings and nobles practiced Buddhism and were patrons of Buddhist culture. Buddhism's close relationship with the ruling class has given it a longer continuous existence here than in any other country in the world. Because the religion virtually died out within India, Sri Lanka's Sangha takes pride in preserving the early form of the monastic Buddhist discipline.

A Buddhist monk meditates in the company of several Bodhisattvas seated in various postures. This room is in the temple of Shwe Dagon Pagoda in Burma, the largest Buddhist temple in the world.

Southeast Asia

The region known as Southeast Asia stretches from Burma to Indonesia. Historically it has been influenced to a great degree by India—so much so that it is often called "Greater India." Indian merchants and monks brought not only religion but also their civilization—writing, arts, and methods of ruling. Buddhism and Hinduism often coexisted in the same areas, along with the preexisting beliefs in animism, the belief that spirits inhabit all things.

Buddhism came to the country known today as Myanmar (Burma) before the Burmese people did. When Asoka's missionaries arrived, the land was inhabited by the Mon people. By the ninth century, when ethnic Burmese moved into the land from the mountains to the north, the Mons were practicing both Hinduism and Buddhism.

The Burmese gradually established their own kingdom. A great Burmese ruler, King Anawrahta (ruled 1044–7), was converted to Buddhism in 1056 by a monk from the neighboring Mon kingdom of Thaton. Anawrahta sent an envoy to Thaton to ask for scriptures of the religion, but was turned down. In a very un-Buddhist manner, Anawrahta invaded Thaton and carried its king and library back to his capital at Pagan. Anawrahta's conversion was a turning point for Buddhism in Burma, beginning a religious tradition that has remained strong to this day. The Burmese people have a proverb: "To be Burmese is to be Buddhist."

In the eleventh century, the Thai people migrated from southern China into today's Thailand. At that time, the region was under the authority of the Khmer king. A Thai ruler, Rama Khamheng (c. 1275–1317), freed the country from the Khmer power. Khamheng became an ardent Buddhist and made Buddhism the state religion. Khamheng's grandson invited monks from Sri Lanka, by then famous for their learning, to come to Thailand to strengthen the purity of the Thai Sangha. From that time on, Thailand has been a staunchly Buddhist country, whose kings have linked their power to the religion.

The Khmer people of Cambodia were also influenced by Indian civilization. From the beginning of the sixth century, Khmer kings ruled a large area from their capital at Angkhor. They devoted much of their wealth to the construction of magnificent monuments and buildings, the most famous of which is the temple called Angkhor Wat, which was probably used by both Hindus and Buddhists. Hinduism remained the stronger of the two religions until King Jayavarman Paramesvara came to the throne in 1327. He embraced Buddhism, and the Cambodians have followed his example ever since.

King Jayavarman had his daughter marry a king named Fa Ngum, who had merged several small states into the country of Laos. Jayavarman urged Fa Ngum to protect Buddhism and to rule his kingdom according to the religion's principles. He sent his son-in-law a statue of the Buddha which came from Sri Lanka. Called the Luang Prabang, the statue was set up in Fa Ngum's capital, which was renamed in its honor. Buddhism has remained the predominant religion of Laos.

Many large seafaring empires were established in the islands that today make up the nation of Indonesia. Here too, Hinduism and Buddhism coexisted; but in the eighth century, Buddhism was adopted by the Sailendra ruling dynasty of the island of Java. Under the Sailendra's sponsorship, mammoth Buddhist temple-monastery complexes were built. Among them—still standing today—is the largest Buddhist monument in the world, Borobodur. At the end of the thirteenth century, Islam arrived on the island. Over time, it became the predominant religion, although a few Buddhists remain.

Along the Silk Road

Northwest of the Indian heartland lies an area that was sometimes called Gandhara, or Bactria. Today it includes northwest India, northern Pakistan, Afghanistan, eastern Iran, and parts of Central Asia. In ancient times this region was a major crossroads between East and West. Here the cultures of India, Persia, and the Greco-Roman West all mingled. Alexander the Great invaded and conquered the region in 326 B.C. When Alexander left, some of his generals remained as governors. The region included the western section of the Silk Road, the ancient trail that led through fearsome deserts and mountains, serving as the land link between China and the West. The name of the road came from the importance of Chinese silk as merchandise carried by the camel caravans that passed along it. But ideas as well as goods were exchanged along the road. The Silk Road became the major route in the northern spread of Buddhism.

After Asoka's death the Maurya Empire declined. In the chaos of that time, the kingdom of Bactria arose between the Oxus River and the Hindu Kush Mountains. Bactria was ruled by Greek descendants of Alexander the Great's soldiers.

King Menander, who ruled Bactria about 155 B.C.E., was afflicted with a sense of spiritual sickness. He searched vainly for some kind of cure. A Buddhist monk, named Nagasena, arrived in the kingdom and brought the remedy. Nagasena explained Buddhist Dharma to Menander, and gained a convert. The record of Nagasena's arguments, called Conversations with Menander, became part of the Buddhist sacred writings.

Menander became an ardent patron of Buddhism. His coinage in later years holds a picture of a wheel, a Buddhist symbol for Dharma. As an old man, he reputedly handed over his kingdom to his son and became a member of the Sangha.

Invaders overran the Bactrian Empire, and control of the territory changed hands many times. Around the middle of the first century of the common era, fierce warriors related to the Huns established the *Kushan Empire*. The Kushans controlled a far larger territory than Menander had. King Kanishka, who ruled in the first and second century, was a fierce warrior. Ruling from his capital Purushapura (today's Peshawar), Kanishka extended his kingdom east to Kathgar, Yarkand, and Khotan—all oases on the Silk Road. Much like Asoka, however, the king experienced a religious crisis and converted to Buddhism.

Kanishka became a great patron of the religion. He had sacred Buddhist writings inscribed on copper plates and displayed in his capital. (Today they survive only in Chinese translations.) From monasteries established during his reign (such as Bamiyan in today's Afghanistan), monks fanned out through Central Asia. They converted kings, translated scriptures into the native languages, and brought the art of writing to the area. The oases of Central Asia became centers of Buddhism, and the arts flourished. In the eighth century, however, Muslim warriors conquered Central Asia. Over time, Buddhism was supplanted by Islam. But by then, Buddhist bhikkus had already gone farther east on the Silk Road, spreading their religion to China and other lands.

China

In the first century of the common era, according to Chinese legend, Ming-ti, a Han emperor of China, had a dream: A huge figure, radiant like the sun, appeared to the emperor. The next day he ordered agents to go west to find the source of his vision. The agents, after much wandering on the Silk Road, came upon two bhikkus with a white horse, a picture of Buddha, and holy Buddhist writings. The bhikkus agreed to return with the agents to Luoyang, China's capital. There the emperor recognized the figure of the Buddha from his dream. He asked the monks to translate their scriptures into Chinese, and they set to work in a building that became known as the White Horse Temple. (Today there is still a White Horse Temple on that site.)

During the Han Dynasty (202 B.C.E.–220 C.E.), China was one of the great civilizations of the world. It had already developed two philosophies that guided its culture. Both had been founded by men who lived at approximately the same time as the Buddha—Confucius and Lao Tzu. Confucius, the founder of Confucianism, described the proper relationships between people, which if followed would bring harmony to society and government. Lao Tzu, on the other hand, believed that harmony was best gained by following the way (the Tao) of nature. Taoism and Confucianism were equally respected by the Chinese, who had no difficulty in accepting separate truths that answered different needs for different areas of life. Buddhism neither contradicted nor replaced either of these philosophies. In time, it was accepted by Chinese as one of the "Three Great Truths."

After the Han Dynasty was overthrown, China was disunited for the next 350 years. During this time of conflict and turmoil, Buddhism's message sank deep roots among the Chinese people. Sanghas were formed, and Indian missionaries came to teach. Translation bureaus were set up to render the Buddhist religious texts into Chinese.

Soon Chinese monks themselves were making the trek to India to bring back precious texts. The journey was hazardous; the monks had to cross deserts and high mountains to reach their destination. Fa-hsien, who traveled for fifteen years (399–414) on his mission, described the terrors of the Gobi Desert: "There are a great many evil spirits and also hot winds; those who encounter them perish to a man. There are neither birds above nor beasts below. Gazing on all sides as far as the eye can reach in order to mark the track, no guidance is to be obtained save from the rotting bones of dead men, which point the way."

About 250 years later, Hsuan-tsang, whom the Chinese call "the prince of pilgrims," made his famous journey to India. Hsuan-tsang entered India through the old kingdom of Bactria. He visited the place in which Kanishka, then still fierce and unconverted, had held a Chinese hostage. Treating his captive with special respect, Kanishka had erected a building to hold him. This dwelling was now a monastery called Serika, which was the Bactrians' word for China. The face of the Chinese prisoner could still be seen painted on the wall. Hsuan-tsang, as the first Chinese visitor to the monastery, was greeted warmly by the monks who explained its history.

Later, while Hsuan-tsang was traveling on the Ganges River, he was captured by pirates who were looking for a victim to sacrifice to a local deity. As they began to make their sacrificial fire, Hsuan-tsang went into deep meditation and a miracle occurred. Suddenly a cyclone blew up and smashed the pirate ship on the shore. The pirates were so terrified that they released Hsuan-tsang.

When Hsuan-tsang arrived at the Bo tree where Siddhartha had achieved enlightenment, he was overcome by emotion. He wept as he thought of his own failings. If he had not been sinful in a previous existence, he might have lived in the perfect days when Buddha was alive. "I wonder," he thought, "in what troubled whirl of birth and death I was caught when Buddha achieved Enlightenment."

Hsuan-tsang visited Nalanda, the great Buddhist university where scholars from many Buddhist lands came to study. He stayed there for five years, studying and debating the finer points of doctrine with other scholars. His description of Nalanda is the best source we have for this great Buddhist center: "From morning to night (the bhikkus) engage in discussion; the old and the younger mutually help one another. Learned men from different cities, who desire to acquire renown...come here and then their wisdom spreads far and wide. For this reason they style themselves Nalanda students, and are honored as a consequence."

Hsuan-tsang returned to China in 645, and received a hero's welcome in Changan, the capital of the Tang Dynasty. He brought back an enormous number of manuscripts and spent the rest of his life translating and teaching. He hastened the development of Chinese branches of Buddhism, and became a genuine folk hero himself. His adventures on his journey became celebrated in art and folklore. The great Chinese novel, *Monkey*, describes in

> ■ *If on the great journey of life a man cannot find one who is better or at least as good as himself, let him joyfully travel alone: a fool cannot help him on his journey.*
> From the **Dhammapada** (5:61)

allegorical fashion his pilgrimage. The novel's mixture of earthy humor and religious philosophy exemplifies the down-to-earth quality of Chinese Buddhism. In addition, the writings of Hsuan-tsang himself provide a vivid picture of Buddhism in Central Asia and India in the seventh century.

The Tang Dynasty (618–927), was a period of Chinese cultural splendor and a high point of Buddhist influence. Buddhism was then at the center of Chinese religious and intellectual life. Most emperors—including the only female "Son of Heaven," Empress Wu—were patrons of the religion. Some rulers maintained "state temples," where Buddhist rituals were performed for the well-being of the country. The monasteries became the most important social-service agencies of their time. The Sangha maintained hospitals, provided aid for the poor, and distributed food in times of famine. In the year 729, a census counted 126,100 monks and nuns.

The Chinese Buddhists were now ready to go beyond translating Indian texts. They began to write interpretations of the Dharma and to develop new schools of Buddhism. The invention of printing, by Buddhist monks, increased the availability of texts and helped to spread the religion further. The very first printed books were collections of Buddhist scriptures.

In the waning years of the Tang Dynasty, however, Buddhism came under attack. Some Confucian scholars criticized it as a foreign import, polluting the true Chinese ways. The Buddhist monasteries, which had grown in wealth and power, excited envy. Because so many men and women had chosen the life of the Sangha, Buddhism was accused of weakening the Confucian ideal of family and the obligation to produce sons. In 845, the emperor ordered the monasteries closed and all monks and nuns to return to regular life. Although Buddhism survived, it went into a decline over the next thousand years. It would never again play as central a role in Chinese life. However, Chinese ideas continued to enrich newer interpretations of Buddhist thought.

China Spreads The Word

The Chinese version of Buddhism, which came from India before A.D. 100 and which was influenced by Confucianism and

Taoism, became important in East Asia during the 300s. It was this version that eventually spread to Korea, Japan, and Vietnam.

Chinese missionaries brought Buddhism to the region of today's northern Vietnam, which was then a part of the Chinese Empire. (For this reason, the Vietnamese form of Buddhism more closely resembles that of China, rather than that of its neighbors, Laos and Cambodia.) Like the Chinese, the Vietnamese blended Buddhism with their native religious practices. Each large village had an image of Buddha, and members of the Sangha took an important part in village affairs. The monks, with their knowledge of medicine and philosophy, were highly respected by the people, and soon they attracted followers among the aristocracy. The Buddhist monks gained popular support by sharing the Vietnamese struggle against Chinese domination and, much later, against French colonial rule.

The peninsula of Korea was frequently under the sway of the *Chinese Empire* as well. By tradition, a Chinese monk named Sundo brought Buddhism to Korea in 372. At that time, there were three Korean kingdoms, and the northern two rapidly accepted the religion. The southernmost, Silla, resisted, and the people there killed a missionary from the north. But this missionary, Yi Chadon, predicted that his blood would run as white as milk to demonstrate the truth of the Buddhist Dharma. When this prophecy came true, the Sillans also accepted the religion. Korean Buddhism experienced a golden age from the sixth to the fourteenth centuries, a time when its kings were patrons of the religion.

In 552, a Korean king sent missionaries to the islands of Japan. They carried to the Japanese court an image of Buddha and a letter from the king, praising the religion as "the most excellent of all teachings....It brings endless and immeasurable blessings and fruits, even the attainment of the supreme enlightenment...the Treasures of the glorious religion will never cease to give full response to those who seek for it."

The letter started a debate in Japan. If the foreign religion were accepted, would it offend the kami? Kami, the Japanese believed, were spirits that inhabited all nature. Simple shrines devoted to the kami dotted the country. Japanese mythology traced the ancestry of their emperor to the Sun Goddess, the most powerful of all kami. It was only after the introduction of Buddhism that these practices were given a name—Shinto, or "the Way of the Gods."

One noble family adopted Buddhism and built a temple for worship. Unfortunately, soon afterward a plague broke out, and the new religion was blamed. The temple was ordered destroyed. But when the plague grew worse, the Buddhists petitioned to rebuild their temple. The argument between the two sides went on.

In 592, Prince Shotoku Taishi became the chief adviser for the Japanese empress, Suiko. Shotoku, an ardent Buddhist convert, urged the empress to adopt the religion. Two years later, Buddhism was proclaimed the state religion. Prince Shotoku began to build a temple complex as a center of Buddhist learning. This was the start of the structure later known as the Horuji, one of Japan's greatest Buddhist shrines.

Japan sent envoys to China to study Buddhist scriptures and learn more about the religion. The mission found more than it had bargained for. It brought back Chinese ideas of culture and government, along with Confucianism and Taosim as well. From that beginning, Japan began to adopt and adapt much that was valuable in Chinese culture, including Buddhism.

Prince Shotoku and his successors began to transform Japan. In 710, a new capital was built at Nara, a city modeled on China's capital, Changan. Many Buddhist monasteries were built within the city, and the emperor Shomu expressed his devotion to Buddhist Dharma. In an imperial decree, Shomu declared: "Our fervent desire is that, under the aegis of the Three Treasures (the Three Jewels), the benefits of peace may be brought to all in Heaven and on earth, even animals and plants sharing in its fruits, for all time to come."

Shomu's daughter, the empress Koken, took steps to unite Buddhism with Shinto. She arranged a ceremony for the Shinto god of war, Hachiman. Buddhist monks and nuns obediently prayed over this god—an unlikely one, since the Buddha preached nonviolence. The monks placed a cap on a sacred cart supposed to contain the spirit of Hachiman. In this ceremony both religions were given equal status in Japan.

■ *School girls on an outing at the Kamakura shrine. Notice the statue of the meditating Buddha (Diabutsu). This temple is famous in Japan because of this colossal Diabutsu.*

The introduction of Buddhism was a spur to Japanese culture. It provided an outlet for the Japanese love of beauty. Buddhism, as the Hachiman ceremony showed, was also a flexible system that could adapt to different ideals, because it stresses the insignificance of things wordly. Indeed, not long after its introduction, Buddhism in Japan would become the favored religion of the samurai warrior class and would be reflected in much of Japanese culture.

Tibet

Now part of China, Tibet, the "Land of Snows," is located in a large plateau of the Himalayas, often called the "Roof of the World." Because of its remote location, Tibet has often been isolated from the rest of the world. The Tibetan indigenous religion, known as bon, was a mixture of magic and animism. The bon-po, a type of shaman, or medicine man, recited mantras, sacred formulas or magical words used to exorcise evil spirits or to call forth powerful forces. In early times bon-pos presided over death rites of the Tibetan kings.

Buddhism first arrived in Tibet in the seventh century when a Tibetan king married a Chinese princess. She was a Buddhist, and brought with her images for which the king built a temple. But Buddhism did not become strongly rooted until the arrival of the Indian Buddhist Padmasambhava a century later.

According to Tibetan tradition, Padmasambhava, or Guru Rinpoche, encountered a series of demons as he made his way toward Tibet. The demons wanted to keep him from ending their hold on the country. Fortunately, Padmasambhava possessed a knowledge of magic and overcame the demons. He did not destroy them (as he might have done in a western tradition). Instead, Padmasambhava forced them to submit to the Dharma and become the new protectors of the religion. The legendary defeat of the demons explains Buddhism's absorption of local religious traditions in Tibet. Padmasambhava established the first Tibetan Buddhist monastery, Samye, completed in 779.

To this day, Padmasambhava is a culture hero in Tibet, celebrated in dance and song. He brought not only the religion that is universally practiced, but also the Tibetan written language. Buddhism became the single most important force in the lives of the Tibetan people. In the centuries that followed, an enormous number of monasteries and temples were built. From Tibet, Buddhism spread farther north into Mongolia.

Ironically, as Buddhism spread throughout Asia, it was fading in the land of its birth. Hinduism was going through a period of regeneration. New sects won greater popular support. On his pilgrimage to India, Hsuan-tsang noted that at Benares, where Buddha preached his first sermon, most of the people were

Hindus. In some areas, the Buddha was worshiped as a reincarnation of Vishnu, one of the Hindu trinity of chief gods. Only in the monasteries was Buddhism a vital force.

The final blow to Indian Buddhism came when Muslims from Afghanistan invaded northern India around the year 1200. They sacked and burned many shrines and monasteries. The great university at Nalanda was destroyed, and the invaders fed its library to the flames for ten days. The great era of Buddhism within its founder's homeland was over.

Today, Buddhist monks live at some of the famous sites of the Buddha's life. They welcome pilgrims from the many lands where Buddhism has taken root. Though the message of the Buddha is still honored by 300 million people in Asia, Buddhism has few followers in the land of its birth.

CHAPTER 4

The Varieties of Buddhism

*T*he Buddha said,"The Dharma which I have taught you will be your teacher when I have gone." Soon after the Buddha's death, his followers gathered in a council to agree on his teachings. A century later, a second council was held. By this time, different viewpoints about the Dharma had started to appear among the Buddhists. As Buddhism spread further and the community grew, two viewpoints took shape, which hardened into a basic split within Buddhism.

One was a conservative approach that desired to hew as closely as possible to the doctrines and practices as originally formulated. This approach was called the School of the Elders or Theravada.

The other group chose to interpret liberally the teachings and practices of the Buddha. By the beginning of the common era, its followers had given it the name Mahayana, which means "great vehicle." Buddha had referred to his teaching as a raft, a vehicle that carried pilgrims across the river to the "other shore." The name Mahayana conveyed the idea that it would carry the whole world to salvation. Mahayanans labeled the Theraveda School as the "lesser vehicle," or Hinayana.

Mahayana Buddhism

At the center of Mahayana Buddhism is the figure of the *bodhisattva*—literally, a "Being of Wisdom." A bodhisattva is a being who is very close to Nirvana, but turns back before reaching it to work for the salvation of all beings. A bodhisattva will delay its Nirvana until even the smallest creature has reached the highest goal. Buddha had been a bodhisattva in his lives (or rebirths) before he was born as Siddartha Gautama.

■ *Statue of Bodhisattva, a Buddhist monk who is on the verge of attaining Nirvana but who vows to refrain from his Nirvana in order to help each and every living being achieve it. From Afganistan, Gandhara style.*

The bodhisattva not only radiates compassion, but even bears the pains and sufferings of others. The vow of the bodhisattva is similar to the sacrificial role of Jesus in Christianity:

I take upon myself...the deeds of all beings, even of those in the hells, in other worlds, in the realm of punishment... I take their suffering upon me...I bear it, I do not draw back from it, I do not tremble at it...I have no fear of it... I must bear the burden of all beings, for I have vowed to save all things living, to bring them safe through the forest of birth, age, disease, death and rebirth. I think not of my own salvation, but strive to bestow on all beings the royalty of supreme wisdom...For it is better that I alone suffer than the multitude of living beings. I give myself in exchange. I redeem the universe from the forest of purgatory, from the womb of flesh, from the realm of death...For I have resolved to gain supreme wisdom for the sake of all that lives, to save the world. (Basham-275)

In short, a bodhisattva is a savior. A bodhisattva gains merit for humankind by practicing the Six Virtues, or Paramitas. A virtue is practiced to perfection when it is carried out with a mind free from self-consciousness, ulterior motives, or self praise.

> ■ *Think not the fault of others, of what they have done or not done. Think rather of your own sins, of the things you have done or not done.*
> From the **Dhammapada** *(4:50)*

The six virtues are:

1. The perfection of giving (dana)
2. The perfection of morality (sila)
3. The perfection of patience (santi)
4. The perfection of courage (virya)
5. The perfection of meditation (dhyana)
6. The perfection of wisdom (prajna)

The bodhisattvas can be reborn as humans or even animals. But the most powerful bodhisattvas are those in heaven. The Mahayana School of Buddhism developed the idea of a heaven, peopled with bodhisattvas who could be adored and petitioned with prayer. The heavens also include past buddhas (enlightened ones) and a Buddha of the Future—Maitreya.

Some bodhisattvas have been more important or beloved than others. Among them are:

Maitreya, the earliest bodhisattva around whom a cult of devotion formed. He answers the prayers of worshipers. A compassionate and benevolent being, he grants help to anyone who calls on him.

Avalokitesvara, who is rich in compassion and love because he has purified his vows for countless eons. He can take any form that will help human beings. He grants rewards and wishes to those who remember him and recite his name. He is the patron of Tibet; and in China, where he was transformed into the female Kwan Yin, he is the most popular of all bodhisattvas.

Manjushri (meaning "sweet" or "gentle"), the symbol of wisdom and eloquence. He is young and never grows old. Manjushri usually appears in dreams, sometimes as an orphan or a poor man. Whoever worships him is protected by the power of Manjushri and is certain to reach enlightenment.

The new development of the bodhisattva as an ideal raised a question about the historical Buddha. Why didn't he remain a bodhisattva instead of selfishly reaching Nirvana and passing from existence? The Mahayana answer to this problem is found in a doctrine called the Three Bodies of the Buddha.

The Buddha's three bodies are the Body of Essence, the Body of Bliss, and the Transformation Body. Living on earth as Siddartha Gautama, the Buddha inhabited the Transformation Body. But his Transformation Body was really an emanation, or manifestation, of his Body of Bliss. In the Body of Bliss, he dwells in the heavens eternally as what might be called a supreme god. The Body of Bliss, in turn, is an emanation of the Body of Essence, which is the Ultimate Buddha. The Ultimate Buddha underlies the entire universe and is identified with Nirvana itself. The Ultimate Buddha or Body of Essence is much like the World Soul or Brahman in Hinduism, presented in a new form.

■ *Kuanyin. In eleventh-century China, the Buddha was transformed into a female Deity of Compassion called Kuanyin.*

Mahayana theology developed the idea that there were other Bodies of Bliss—all emanations of the single Body of Essence. These Bodies of Bliss were identified as bodhisattvas and "other" buddhas, who had lived at various times in past history. These figures multiplied into a pantheon of beings who dwelled in numerous heavens, hells, and even other universes. Mahayana Buddhist thinkers envisioned wonderful paradises and their counterpart hells, where the wicked suffered horrible punishments. The only limit to new creations was the human imagination.

The concept of the Bodies of Bliss allowed Mahayana Buddhism to absorb the gods and historical figures of other lands. For example, in China, Taoist sages (saintly wise men) were incorporated into Mahayana forms as buddhas (and bodhisattvas), as was the Japanese goddess Amaterasu, the most important spirit in the Shinto pantheon.

The most beloved Bodies of Bliss, however, were those concerned with life and sufferings here on earth. The most important were the Buddha Amitabha ("Immeasurable Radiance"), who resided in the heaven of the West. He was linked with the historical Buddha Gautama and the very powerful and compassionate bodhisattva Avalokitesvara, whose name means "the Lord Who Looks Down."

Mahayana theology was buttressed by two primary philosophical schools. The first school was the Madyamika, or Doctrine of the Middle Position. It was developed by Nagarjuna, who lived in the first and second centuries of the common era. Nagarjuna postulated that all that exists is emptiness, or *the Void* (Sunyata). For this reason his theory is sometimes called the doctrine of emptiness. Nagarjuna admitted that for practical purposes the everyday world existed. But because it was composed of transitory or impermanent phenomena, it had no absolute reality. Since emptiness is the only phenomenon that never changes, the Void is absolute reality. The Void, in fact, is the same as Nirvana and the Body of Essence of the Buddha.

The Madyamika doctrine included a very optimistic corollary. Although the existence of emptiness could not be proved by ordinary logic, it could be directly experienced in meditation. The emptiness or Void was everywhere: indeed, there was no difference between the ultimate Void and the world of phenomena. Humans and all beings were already part of the emptiness or Void. Potentially, they were all buddhas if they could only, through meditation, recognize the Void and realize the true nature of things.

The Madyamika doctrine was popular in China and Japan. Because it emphasized salvation in the real world, it appealed to the practical spirit of the Chinese and Japanese. Since the real world and Nirvana were the same, Madyamika appealed to the love of nature that was an important value in both countries. Indeed, portrayal of the Void became important in Chinese and Japanese art. Moreover, the Madyamika doctrine offered a quicker path to enlightenment. The need for rebirths was less important, for Nirvana or Buddhahood were omnipresent and only needed to be realized.

The second philosophical school, called Yogacara, was founded in the fourth century. Its central belief is that the phenomenal world exists only in the mind of the beholder. It uses as an example the monk who in meditation can conjure up visions that are as real as his ordinary perception of the mundane world. Yet the monk knows that they are a product of his own thoughts. The only independent reality outside the mind, according to the Yogacara School, is an entity called Suchness. Suchness (Tathagata) is without characteristics, pure and whole. It is the counterpart of the Void of the Madyamikas.

Salvation in the Yogacara School came from purifying oneself until one reached the state of absolute purity, or Suchness. The purifying process was a rigorous one and only those at a high state of spiritual development could achieve it. Basically, the meditating person conjured up visions that were as vivid as possible, absorbing their reality. Through constant practice, the subjectivity of the perceptions of the everyday world and his visions would be apparent. The adept would realize that all phenomena were subjective. Only when the visions and ordinary phenomena were perceived in the same manner was Suchness reached.

The ideas of Mahayana Buddhism created a religion of two levels. For the intellectual, the intricate underpinnings provided a challenging and creative philosophy. However, at the popular level, Mahayana Buddhism offered something more concrete—devotion to the buddhas and bodhisattvas. The knowledge that they were working for the salvation of all beings was comforting. Moreover, these heavenly beings heard prayers and appeals directly from those in need, and acted as personal saviors.

Differences Between Theravada and Mahayana Buddhism

Although both Theravada and Mahayana Buddhism recognized Siddartha Gautama as the founder of the religion, their differences were profound. These differences can be summarized in nine points.

  1. The ideal of the *arhat* and the ideal of the bodhisattva. In Theravada Buddhism the ideal was the arhat. The arhat was a person, usually a monk, who through the Eightfold

Path became an enlightened one, and thus experienced Nirvana. His aim was single-mindedly to reach enlightenment for himself. In Mahayana Buddhism, the bodhisattva postpones personal Nirvana to work for the salvation of all beings.

2. The goal of Nirvana and the goal of Buddhahood. In Theravada Buddhism, the goal was to attain Nirvana through the Eightfold Path. The goal for the Mahayana Buddhist was the attainment of Buddhahood itself. The Theravadins recognized a difference between the achievement of the Buddha, which was the highest possible, and the attainment of Nirvana by an arhat. In Mahayana, anyone could in theory reach buddhahood.

3. The role of self-effort and the role of faith in achieving the goal of salvation. The Theravadins demanded that Nirvana be achieved through the efforts of the individual alone. Mahayana Buddhists permitted the use of prayers and faith, and the help of the buddhas and bodhisattvas, as part of the process of salvation.

4. The historical Buddha and many buddhas. The Theravadins stressed the importance of the historical Buddha whose greatness lay in his Dharma. Although they regarded him as the highest specimen of humanity, they did not regard him as divine. In Mahayana Buddhism, the historical Buddha was one of many buddhas and bodhisattvas. He was identified with the Supreme Essence and thus had attributes of a god.

5. The monks and the laity. Theravada Buddhism has been called a religion of monks. The Sangha was the center of the religious community. The laity gained merit through serving the Sangha by providing food and donations in return for its precious teaching. In Mahayana Buddhism, the Sangha was important as a preserver and teacher of Buddhist tradition and learning. But the laity had a larger role; they could pray directly to the bodhisattvas and could seek salvation directly through them.

6. The relative importance of wisdom and compassion. The highest attribute of Theravada Buddhism is wisdom. The attainment of it brings the goal of Nirvana. In Mahayana Buddhism, the highest attribute is compassion—to bring the whole chain of being to salvation.

7. Pali and Sanskrit scriptures. Both branches of Buddhism claim that their scriptures or sutras are the direct teachings of the Buddha, transmitted orally for generations before being written. The Theravada scriptures were first written down in Sri Lanka in the first century B.C.E. They are in

■ *North Vietnamese Buddhist nuns march in front of the Golden Shwe Da Pagoda in Rangoon, Burma, in protest against the South Vietnamese government's persecution of Buddhist monks and nuns in South Vietnam.*

Pali, an ancient Indian language. The Mahayana scriptures were written down later in the Sanskrit language. They contain some of the same literature as the Theravada texts, but have an enormous library of their own. Mahayana Buddhists believe that their new sutras were given by the Buddha to specially chosen disciples.

8. One school and many schools. Theravada has only one school of religious thought. Its followers claim that this is the same one that the historical Buddha taught in his lifetime. The Mahayana branch of Buddhism has many schools. Their liberal interpretation of Buddhism was more open to new schools of thought, which are constantly evolving.

9. Spread by southern route or northern route. The Theravada branch of Buddhism spread to the south. The countries of Sri Lanka, Burma, Thailand, Laos, and Cambodia all practice Theravada Buddhism. Mahayana Buddhism arose in the northwest of India. According to tradition, King Kanishka convoked a Buddhist council at which sutras were written down. Mahayana Buddhism spread from northwest India across Asia to China, Korea, and Japan.

The Pure Land Sect

When the Chinese first encountered Buddhism, they had no idea of the split within it. They took the different scriptures as they obtained them, piecemeal. As the pilgrimages described in the previous chapter show, the first phase of Chinese Buddhism included attempts to obtain as many texts as possible.

Later the Chinese made their own contributions to Buddhist doctrine. First, Chinese scholars enriched the religion by adding commentaries to Mahayana scriptures. Hsuan-tsang, for example, devoted himself to the Yogacara School and wrote commentaries, or interpretations, of its texts. Other scholars synthesized the vast number of Mahayana writings into a single coherent system.

The Chinese also developed the Meditation School. In this tradition, the techniques of meditation superseded the need for scriptures. These Chinese contributions were important because it was Chinese Buddhism that spread to Vietnam, Korea, and Japan—where new forms, traditions, and practices were subsequently added.

But the Chinese contribution went beyond scholarly commentaries and techniques. Chinese religious leaders developed everyday methods of devotion that helped to make Buddhism a popular religion in East Asia. An example was the Pure Land Sect, which centers around the Buddha Amitabha.

The Buddha Amitabha ("the Buddha of Boundless Light"), is one of the most beloved of the "new" buddhas of Mahayana Buddhism. Buddhists believe that in a former time, eons ago, when Amitabha was on the verge of enlightenment, he made a vow: When he had attained his goal, if there were any "beings in other worlds" who heard his name and thought upon him favorably, then he would help them. If he did not keep this vow, then he prayed that he would not attain enlightenment at all.

Since Amitabha did in fact become a buddha, the truth of his vow was assured. Thus, people could call on his help at any time.

The paradise in which Amitabha dwells is called the Pure Land. In this place of splendor, the leaves and flowers of the trees are precious stones of all colors. On its waters grow lotuses larger than any on earth. Birds sing continually, the clouds pour forth music, and chimes tinkle in the breeze from the trees. Those who follow Amitabha can someday reach this Pure Land.

In China, where Amitabha is called A-mi-t'o-fo, the Pure Land Sect developed in the seventh century. Devout Pure Land Buddhists believe that if they call on the name of Amida (the Japanese form of the name Amitabha), he will lead them to the Pure Land after their deaths. This simple belief brought great comfort from the sufferings of the world. Over time, the simple invocation of his name became the most popular religious practice in China. In religious art, A-mi-t'o-fo was depicted sitting on his Lotus Throne, often flanked by Kwan Yin, China's favorite bodhisattva.

The Chinese monk Honen (1133–1212) carried the Pure Land sect to Japan. He arrived there during a time of turmoil, when competing military leaders waged war on each other. Honen's answer to the disorder and suffering was total dependence on the compassion of Amida.

The call to Amida was not new to Japanese Buddhism. Honen, however, made it the essential element of his preaching. The repetition of the phrase, "Namu Amida Butsu" ("Hail to Lord Buddha Amida") was all that was required for salvation. A text of the Pure Land Sect declares:

> The mere repetition (of the phrase) with firm faith
> includes all the practical details....Those who believe
> this, though they clearly understand all the teachings
> Shaka (the historical Buddha) taught throughout his
> whole life, should behave themselves like simple-minded
> folk, who know not a single letter, or like ignorant
> nuns or monks whose faith is implicitly simple. Thus
> without pedantic airs, they should fervently practice
> the repetition of the name of Amida, and that alone.
> (de Bray-202)

Shinran, a monk and a disciple of Honen, carried his teacher's ideas even further. He declared that the mere expression of the phrase only once in a lifetime brought salvation. In a shocking gesture, Shinran took a wife, thus breaking his monastic vow of chastity. He argued that since the grace of Amida was all that mattered, the discipline of monastic vows was unimportant. He claimed that the family and the home were the proper setting for religious life. Shinran organized his followers into the True Pure Land sect, and it is today the most popular Buddhist group in Japan.

The Meditation School

Another school of Mahayana Buddhism that developed in China was the *Ch'an* (Meditation) School. Meditation has always been important to Buddhism. The Buddha himself, sitting under the Bo Tree, reached enlightenment through meditation. The Meditation School, however, found special meaning in Buddha's advice: "Look within, thou art the Buddha."

The arrival in China in 520 of Bodhidharma, an Indian missionary monk, launched the Ch'an school. By tradition,

Bodhidharma came to China to restore the original spirit of the religion. On his arrival, he met the Chinese emperor, who described all the things he had done to promote the religion. The emperor asked Bodhidharma, "What merit have I earned from my acts?" Bodhidharma replied, "None whatsoever." The emperor then asked what Bodhidharma regarded as the first principle of Buddhism. "Vast emptiness," said Bodhidharma.

Bodhidharma then retreated to a monastery, where he stayed for nine years. During all that time he constantly meditated while staring at a blank wall. It is said that when his eyelids started to droop from fatigue, Bodhidharma cut them off and cast them aside. In the places where they fell, tea plants grew. Tea's original popularity was as a stimulant that helped keep Buddhist monks awake during meditation.

The Ch'an School put meditation at the center of its religious practice. Meditation was not only a method or means of intuiting the Body of Essence, but the only way. Indeed, meditation was more than a means—it was believed to be the Truth realized in action. In pursuit of this goal, followers felt free to give up the study of scripture to pursue an intuitive approach to enlightenment. The techniques of meditation were passed from master to disciple in a completely personal transmission of insights.

The Ch'an School was influenced by the two indigenous Chinese philosophies. Confucianism and Taosim taught that humans were basically good. People only needed guidance and support to tap their essential wisdom. Confucius taught that people should keep their minds on the here and now. Taoists taught that people should follow their own nature. "Everything is what it is," and understanding this was a form of enlightenment. To increase intuition, Taoists had often used riddles and paradoxes. Ch'an Buddhism combined this technique with a down-to-earth outlook. In addition, in a break with tradition, the monks were required to perform physical labor.

The Chinese Meditation School developed the kung-an (koan in Japanese). This was a paradoxical statement to shake up the mind. A master would tell his pupils puzzling tales whose point was obscure. Or, the master might pose a series of seemingly unanswerable questions. (An example is, "What is the sound of one hand clapping?") While the pupil meditated on these stories or questions, masters would often do something to shock them. They might shout into the pupil's ear, or even give them a sharp blow with a stick. The purpose of this was to jolt the pupil into a state that embraced both the world of meditation and the physical world. Combining them both at once would make the pupil aware of the true nature of things. They would thus achieve the Suchness goal of Yogacara philosophy.

The Meditation School spread to Korea and Vietnam, but it had its greatest influence in Japan. Known there as *Zen*, it combined the mystic conceptions of the Indian version with the down-to-earth approach and techniques of the Chinese. The goal was to use meditation to reach *Satori* or enlightenment. Zen Buddhism had two main schools. Both were transmitted to Japan in the twelfth and early thirteenth century.

Eisai was a Japanese monk who was discouraged by what he considered the staleness of religion in Japan. He journeyed to China for further study and there became attracted to Ch'an. After achieving enlightenment, Eisai returned to Japan as a Zen master. He set up his school, called the Rinzai, and soon attracted disciples. The Rinzai used koans as an aid to cleanse the mind for meditation. Thinking about them could bring one to the state of readiness for Satori. Eisai claimed for his doctrine, "Outwardly it favors discipline over doctrine, inwardly it brings the Highest Inner Wisdom."

Dogen, the second founder of Japanese Zen, established the Soto school. Dogen's followers used zazen meditation as the way to reach Satori. Zazen was sitting (za) meditation (zen). A follower of Dogen described the process:

> In a place, which must be quiet, spread a thick cushion
> and sit yourself on it in an upright posture. Now first
> swell out the abdomen and put your strength there.
> Let the shoulders be in a straight line below the ears,
> and navel below the nose. Make the spine straight.
> The mouth should be shut, but you may have the eyes
> slightly opened. Making the breath flow gently
> will help you to secure a correct posture. Then meditate
> on the text you have been given, or in the case of

> ■ *If a man tries not to learn he grows old just like an ox! His body indeed grows old but his wisdom does not grow.*
> From the **Dhammapada** (11:152)

beginners there is a method in which they count their
breaths and so remove dull and distracted thoughts.
So entering the Samadhi or undisturbed purity, remain
in the meditation. (Conze 134-135)

Both Zen sects shared many beliefs and practices. Each revered the historic Buddha. In both, the training went from a master to his disciples. Each sect believed that within each person it was possible to awaken the Buddha mind. Both argued that religious devotion was expressed in daily work.

Zen became the religion of the warrior class in Japan. The warriors, or samurai, were attracted by a religion where it was not necessary to study philosophical texts or to observe ritual. It was simple and emphasized discipline, a trait honored by the warrior. Zen was also the inspiration for many of the distinctive arts of Japan.

Tantric Buddhism

Around the fifth century C.E., a new variety of Buddhism arose in India. It is called *Vajrayana*, or Tantric Buddhism. The two names reveal the unusual nature of its relationship to Mahayana Buddhism. The word Vajrayana ("The Thunderbolt" or "Diamond Vehicle") implies that it is a whole new branch of Buddhism. The thunderbolt is a symbol of Ultimate Reality, or the Void. But Mahayana philosophy underlies Vajrayana, although the latter used a new technique to attain salvation—the *tantra*.

Tantra is the name of manuals or guidebooks that contain the techniques for gaining enlightenment. *Tantrism* developed a system of beliefs and practices understood only by adepts, called gurus, who were skilled in the use of the manuals. The tantras included magic spells (mantras), occult diagrams (mandalas), and symbolic hand gestures (mudras).

Tantric methods were practiced by Hindus and Buddhists alike. Their goal was to reach a mystical union with reality beyond everyday reality. This was symbolized in Hinduism as the union between a god and his consort. In Buddhism the union was between bodhisattvas or buddhas and a feminine partner. Through meditation the devotee reached an inner unity with the buddha or bodhisattva and experienced bliss and Ultimate Reality.

Vajrayana became part of the Buddhism of Nepal, China, and Japan. But its greatest development and elaboration took place in Tibet. By tradition, the Indian monk Padmasambhava introduced Tantrism to Tibet. In Tibet, a guru was called a lama. A lama need not be a monk—his skills in the tantra were all that mattered. The lama assumed such importance in Tibet that the religion is often called Lamaism.

The highest duty of the lama was to guide a dying person as the spirit left his body. For forty-nine days, the spirit would exist in *bardo*, the state between after death and rebirth. During this time, the instructions given by the lama would help the spirit reach either enlightenment or rebirth.

In the eleventh century, a Tibetan guru, Mar-pa (1012–1096), renewed the Tantric tradition after studying in India. Marpa was a married householder who led the ordinary life of a farmer. Yet he translated the Sanskrit writings of Buddhism and gathered disciples, to whom he revealed the secrets and practices of tantrism he had learned in India. Spritually, he claimed descent from a buddha called Vajradhara ("Holder of the Vajra").

Mar-pa's most famous disciple was Mi-la-ras-pa (1012–1135). For many years, Mi-la-ras-pa meditated in caves in the high Himalaya Mountains, practicing and developing the techniques he had learned from Mar-pa. His powers included the ability to develop internal heat, so that even in the bitterly cold winters of the world's highest mountains, he wore only a thin robe of white cotton.

Neither Mar-pa nor Mi-la-ras-pa was ever ordained as a monk. They were important in Tibetan Buddhism for creating poetry to express their personal religious experiences. This began a tradition that has continued in Tibet to modern times.

Toward the end of the twelfth century, waves of Indians entered Tibet, fleeing the Muslim invaders who devastated northern India. Before this time, Tibetan pilgrims had gone to India for spiritual learning. Now, Tibetans began to see their own country as the spiritual center of Buddhism. They believed that the Buddha himself had prophesied this destiny. The bodhisattva Avaloki-tesvara began to be revered as the patron of the Tibetan state.

In the fifteenth century, a religious leader named Tsong-kha-pa established the Ge-luk-pa School. It was important for two reasons. First, the Ge-luk-pa became the dominant school in Tibetan Buddhism. Tsong-kha-pa founded monasteries near Lhasa, the capital, and made that city the center of his religious group.

The second reason was that the third successor of Tsong-kha-pa was the first *Dalai Lama* ("Ocean of Wisdom"). He and his successors are believed to be reincarnations of Avalokitesvara. For centuries afterward, on the death of the Dalai Lama, a search began for the child who was his latest incarnation. Once found, the child was educated by the elder lamas in preparation for his role. In 1642, a converted Mongol chief placed the Dalai Lama on the throne of Tibet, making him both the temporal and religious leader of the country, a position that endured until 1959, when the Chinese Communist government took control of Tibet.

Tibetan doctrine recognizes three vehicles to reach the final goal of Buddhism. The methods take into account the different levels of spiritual development of the practitioners. The first of these methods is the Theravada, which through self-discipline brings the devotee to the goal of self-emancipation. Many monks practice this discipline. The second is the Mahayana, which is the path to philosophical insight for the sake of saving others. The third is the Vajrayana, which is the way of tantric rites and mystical meditations. At a higher level these three disciplines are seen as successive steps in the One Vehicle (Ekayana). The lamas spend fourteen to twenty years studying the first two vehicles before they are ready for the tantras. These books set forth the rituals, mystical meditation, and spells that can lead to Supreme Wisdom. Only specially qualified masters can lead the adept through this phase. Tibet's three ways have made the country a virtual museum of Buddhism.

■ *A **Vajrayana** prayer bell with a spear handle*

CHAPTER 5

The Literature
of Buddhism

Near the summit of Mt. Kaya in Korea, nestled amidst cascading mountain streams and a grove of trees, is one of Buddhism's most famous shrines—the Haein Temple complex. "The impermanence of all things" is marked by the brief appearance of cherry blossoms in spring and the brilliant foliage of flaming maples and golden oaks in the fall. Thousands of visitors come each year to the ninety-three wooden structures that include a monastery where monks chant Buddhist sutras day and night.

Yet the most important part of the Haein Temple is its library, housed in two buildings that are nearly 600 years old. They contain over 80,000 wooden blocks that were originally used to print copies of the Buddhist scriptures on rice paper.

The blocks were carved on the order of King Kojong of Korea in the fourteenth century. At the time, Mongol invaders occupied his country, and the king sponsored the project to ensure divine favor for the Koreans. Over a sixteen-year period, a total of 81,258 woodblocks were completed. Each birchwood block, carved on both sides, measures about nine by twenty-seven inches.

The Koreans succeeded in driving out the Mongols, and the precious woodblocks were housed in the Haein Temple, near today's city of Taegu. Because the wood was specially treated to prevent decay, the blocks have survived to the present day. They make up the world's largest single collection of Buddhist scriptures.

As followers of the Mahayana tradition, the Koreans preserved its written forms. However, even this vast collection contains only part of the complete Buddhist canon. Both Theravada and Mahayana Buddhism have some scriptures in common. But as Mahayana Buddhism spread, its literature greatly expanded. Today the combined writings of the many Buddhist traditions is more extensive than that of any other world religion.

Buddhism never had a single book such as the Bible or the Koran that all its believers accepted. Many schools of Buddhism concentrated on just one scripture as their guide, but later schools have added their own scriptures. Certain works, however, even if in different languages and slightly varied forms, are beloved by all Buddhists. The Buddhist scriptures are a treasure of wisdom that are an important spiritual record of humankind.

The Three Baskets

For five hundred years after the death of the Buddha, his followers memorized and recited his teachings. After the Parinirvana, the Sangha met to agree on the teachings of the Buddha. They preserved them orally, even though India had a written language. For in the Indian tradition, the actual speaking of the sacred words had a special value. The fact that most of the canon was in verse form and used standard opening phrases made memorization easier.

As the years passed, and differences crept into the religion, there was a greater need to commit the Buddha's teachings to writing. The first written Buddhist scriptures were recorded on palm leaves shortly after 43 B.C.E. in Ceylon. Written in the Pali language, they became the scriptural basis for Theravada Buddhism. They are called the Tipitaka, which means "three baskets"— for the texts, which were divided into three categories, were often literally stored in baskets.

The first basket is the Vinaya Pitaka, or "Basket of Discipline." These writings concern the Sangha. They give Buddha's rules of discipline for the monks and nuns. In addition, they provide information on the founding and history of the early monasteries.

The second part of the Tipitaka is the Sutta Pitaka, or "Basket of Discourses." This basket includes the suttas (sutras in Sanskrit), or sermons and stories of the Buddha and his earliest disciples. In these, the Buddha describes his doctrine and the practices necessary to reach Nirvana. The Sutta Pitaka contains many of the most popular works of Buddhism. One of these is the last sermon of Buddha, called "Lamp Unto Yourself." It concludes:

> *Therefore, O Ananda, be ye lamps unto yourselves.*
> *Be ye a refuge to yourselves. Betake yourselves to*
> *no external refuge. Hold fast to the truth as a lamp.*
> *Hold fast as a refuge to the truth. Look not for refuge*
> *to anyone besides yourselves....* (Alphonso-Karkala-238)

This second basket includes the Theripatha—songs of devotion by the first Buddhist nuns. The Theripatha is the world's earliest collection of sacred poetry by women. Among its authors was the Buddha's aunt, his foster mother, Mahaprajapati.

The third basket is the Abhiddhamma Pitaka, or "Basket of Metaphysics." It contains commentaries on the teachings of Buddhism.

Later—by tradition at a council called by King Kanishka in the second century C.E.—Mahayana Buddhists collected their writings in Sanskrit. Called the Tripitaka, this collection is divided into the same categories and contains some of the same works as the Tipitaka. However, the Mahayana Buddhists claim that the Tripitaka contains doctrine that the Buddha revealed only to his most spiritually advanced followers.

Among the important works in the Mahayana Tripitaka is the Lotus Sutra. Like the Judeo-Christian Testaments, the Lotus Sutra is great literature. Its author, supposedly the Buddha himself, employs a wealth of images and parables to teach its message. One story is similar to the Biblical parable of the Prodigal Son. The theme of the Lotus Sutra is universal salvation and the attainment of Buddahood by all believers. In East Asia, many Buddhists believe that the Lotus Sutra embraces and harmonizes the full spectrum of Buddhism.

The Jatakas

Among the most beloved works found in both the Tipitaka and the Tripitaka are the Jataka Tales. In these stories, the Buddha tells about his former lives. By tradition, the Buddha recalled all of his 550 previous states of existence while he attained enlightenment under the Bo tree.

Some of the most charming Jataka Tales describe his adventures in earlier rebirths when he took the form of an animal. The Buddha used these tales to explain his doctrine simply. The Jataka Tales remain popular today and have inspired Asian drama and art for centuries.

Each story begins with an event that caused the Buddha to relate it. In "The Hare Jataka," the Buddha and 500 of his followers arrive at the home of a devout layman, described as "a landowner of Savatthi." For seven days, the landowner treats them to the hospitality of his house.

At the end of the week, the Buddha praises the landowner for his generosity, saying that the "wise men of old lay down their lives for the beggars they met." Asked to tell about the past, the Buddha begins the tale.

A hare lived in a forest at the foot of the mountains, next to a river and a small town. The hare had three companions, an otter, a jackal, and a monkey. By looking at the moon, the hare saw that the next day would be a holy day. He taught his companions that they should fast and prepare to give food to any passing beggar.

The next day, the otter went to the river and smelled a string of seven red fish that a fisherman had buried in the sand. He dug them up and asked loudly, "Does anyone own these?" But since the fisherman had gone downstream, no one answered and the otter took the fish to his lair, saying, "In due time I'll eat them."

The jackal found in the hut of a field watchman two spits of meat, a lizard, and a pot of milk. He too called for the owner, but when no one appeared dragged them back to his lair, thinking, "In due time I'll eat them."

The monkey picked a bunch of mangoes from a tree in the forest, and placed them in his lair, saying, "In due time I'll eat them."

The hare went out and thought to gather grass to eat. But he realized that if a beggar came by, grass would not be a sufficient meal. "I have no rice nor oil," thought the hare. "So if a beggar comes to me I will give him my own flesh."

This resolution was so virtuous that it warmed the throne of Sakka in heaven. He disguised himself as a Brahmin and went to earth. First he came to the otter, who offered him the seven red fish. The Brahmin promised to come back on the next day. Then he went to the jackal, who offered the meat, lizard, and milk. Again the Brahmin said he would return. The same thing happened at the monkey's lair.

Finally the Brahmin came to the hare. The hare said, "You did well in coming to me for food. For I will give a gift that I have never given before. But you, as a moral man, will not have to take life. Go and make a fire and when it is ready I will leap into it and when my body is roasted you may eat my flesh."

The Brahmin used his supernatural powers to make a fire. The hare remembered that there might be insects in his fur, so he shook himself three times so that they would not be killed. Then he jumped into the fire. But he lay there as if he had entered a cave of snow.

"Brahmin," said the hare, "the fire you have made isn't even able to heat the fur on my body. How is this?"

"Wise man, I am not a Brahmin. I am Sakka come to test you."

The hare said, "Your efforts are useless, for if all the beings in the world would test my generosity, they would not find me unwilling to give."

"Wise hare," said Sakka, "let your virtue be proclaimed to the end of the world-cycle." Sakka took a mountain and squeezed juice from it, and with the juice drew the outline of a hare on the moon. Then he placed the hare on a nest of soft grass and departed for his celestial abode.

The hare and his friends lived happily and virtuously and passed away according to their deeds.

Having finished the tale, the Buddha revealed that in this existence, the otter was Ananda, the jackal and monkey were two other of his followers, and the hare "was I myself." (adapted from Stories of the Buddha, ed. Caroline Rhys Davids)

The Way of Righteousness

No Buddhist scripture is more widespread than the Way of Righteousness (the Dhammapada in Pali; the Dharmapada in Sanskrit). It is a source of wisdom and comfort to all Buddhists. The Way of Righteousness is a selection of the brief sayings that the Buddha made during his forty-five years of teaching. There are 423 verses arranged in twenty-six chapters under such topics as friendship, thought, earnestness, punishment and evil.

The following selection gives a brief sample.

1. All that we are is the result of what we have thought: it is founded on our thoughts, it is made up of our thoughts. If a man speaks or acts with an evil thought, pain follows him, as the wheel follows the foot of the ox that draws the carriage.

2. All that we are is the result of what we have thought: it is founded on our thoughts, it is made up of our thoughts. If a man speaks or acts with a pure thought, happiness follows him, like a shadow that never leaves him.

   He who always greets and constantly reveres the aged, four things will increase to him: life, beauty, happiness, power.

129. All men tremble at punishment, all men fear death; remember that you are like unto them, and do not kill, nor cause slaughter.

135. Not nakedness, not plaited hair, not dirt, not fasting, or lying on the earth, not rubbing with dust, not sitting motionless, can purify a mortal who has not overcome desires.

252. The fault of others is easily perceived, but that of one's self is difficult to perceive; a man winnows his neighbors'

faults like chaff, but his own fault he hides, as a cheat hides the bad dice from the player.

277. "All created things perish." He who knows and sees this becomes passive in pain; this is the way to purity.

278. "All created things are grief and pain." He who knows this becomes passive in pain; this is the way to purity.

279. "All forms are unreal." He who knows and sees this becomes passive in pain; this is the way that leads to purity.

334. The thirst of a thoughtless man grows like a creeper; he runs from life to life, like a monkey seeking fruit in the forest.

A Philosophical Exchange

The conversion of King Menander (also known as King Milinda) by Nagasena was a milestone in the spread of Buddhism. It also produced an important text of Buddhist literature—The Milindapanha, or "Questions of Milinda (Menander)." The Milindapanha is written as a dialogue between the two historical figures. King Menander asks Nagasena to explain puzzling or difficut Buddhist ideas. Nagasena's answers, often in story form, are used by Buddhist teachers today to illustrate key points of the Dharma. For example:

King Menander asked, "Why are men different in their natures? Some are long-lived, sickly, ugly or weak, while others are the opposite."

Nagasena's response is used to explain Karma. He replied: "Why is it that all vegetables are not alike, but some sour, and some salt, and some pungent, and some acid, and some astringent, and some sweet?"

"I fancy, Sir, it is because they come from different kinds of seeds."

"And just so, great king, are the differences you have mentioned among men to be explained. For it has been said by the Blessed One: 'Beings, O Brahmin, have each their own Karma, are inheritors of Karma, belong to the tribe of their Karma, are relatives by Karma, have each their Karma as their protecting overlord.

It is Karma that divides them up into high and low and the like divisions.'"

"Very good, Nagasena!"

Similarly, the king asked Nagasena what it was that is reborn.

"Name-and-form," said Nagasena.

This answer surprised the king. "The same name-and-form is reborn?"

"No," said Nagasena. "But by this name-and-form deeds are done, good and evil, and by these deeds (Karma), another name-and-form is reborn."

"If that is so," said the king, "would not the new being be released from its evil Karma?"

Only if it were not reborn, said Nagasena. "But just because it is reborn, O king, it is therefore not released from its evil Karma."

Nagasena gave several illustrations. For example, he said, a man lights a lamp to eat his evening meal. The lamp sets the thatch roof of the house on fire. The fire spreads to other houses until the whole village is burned.

The villagers blame the man with the lamp for setting their homes on fire. But the man replies that it was not the flame from his lamp, but another fire that burned their houses. "How would your majesty decide such a case?"

The king said he would rule in favor of the villagers, because the flame that destroyed the village was produced by the flame from the lamp.

"Just so, great king," said Nagasena, "it is one name-and-form which has its end in death, and another name-and-form which is reborn. But the second is the result of the first, and is therefore not set free from its evil deeds." This was the meaning of Karma.

The Lotus Sutra

The Saddharma-Pundarika, or "The Lotus of the True Law," is one of the most important sutras of Mahayana Buddhism. In it, the historical Buddha teaches a disciple named Sariputra. The sutra is a justification of the additional features of Buddhism that appeared in the Mahayana forms of the religion. Among these are the "lesser vehicles," such as the bodhisattvas.

The acceptance of these "lesser vehicles" as part of Buddhism is one of the differences between Mahayana and Theravada Buddhism. Theravada followers teach only the Buddha's original, stricter dharma, the "Great Cart" of the parable. The Mahayana author of the Lotus Sutra has the Buddha justifying the use of "lesser vehicles" as a way to assist all living beings toward spiritual perfection, or Buddhahood. To illustrate this principle, the Buddha relates the Parable of the Burning House.

Buddha asked Sariputra to imagine an old and wealthy man who owns a great house. The house is old, "the bases of its pillars rotten, the coverings and plaster of the walls loose." It has only one door. Within live the man's many small children.

One day the house catches on fire, and the owner escapes through the door. But he realizes that the children inside are not aware of the danger. The owner wishes to save them. Because he is strong, he considers carrying them through the door. But the door is small, and it may be difficult to gather the children together, for they are running around in all parts of the house.

Instead, the householder calls out to them, warning of the danger. But they do not heed his cries, for they are too young to understand even the meaning of "burning."

The householder knows that the children love to play with toys. So he tells them that he has three toy carts outside for them to play with. Hearing this, they rush toward the doorway, each trying to be the first one through it.

Outside, however, the householder gives them something different. He is a rich man and gives each of them a real cart, drawn by bullocks and swift as the wind. He thinks, "Why should I give these children inferior carts, since they are precious to me?"

"Now, Sariputra," asked the Buddha, "is that man guilty of a falsehood by first holding out to his children the prospect of three vehicles and afterwards giving to each of them the greatest vehicles only?"

"No," answered Sariputra, "for it was only a skillful device to persuade his children to go out of the burning house and save their lives."

Buddha replied that the householder is like the Buddha himself, who found a way out of this world of suffering and pain.

Having saved himself, he wished to save his children as well. But they are ignorant and think of enjoying themselves in the world. So he tells them of the three lesser vehicles. Attracted by them, the children will acquire the knowledge of the Four Noble Truths—the one single grand cart that will take them to Nirvana.

Chinese Dedication Messages

Buddhism flourished in China during the Tang Dynasty. Scholars developed new Buddhist schools of thought, which acquired distinctively Chinese features. Philosophical disputes, however, offered little to the ordinary person. As in the Lotus Sutra, people were attracted to Buddhism by "lesser vehicles," although the essential spirit of the Buddha persisted.

One way a person could gain merit was by paying to have copies made of the scriptures and sutras. In many of the copy-texts, a dedication message explained the motivation of the person who paid for it. These messages show the meaning and comfort Buddhism brought to ordinary Chinese.

Here are two examples: Happiness is not fortuitous; pray for it and it will respond. Results are not born of thin air; pay heed to Buddhism, causes and results will follow. This explains how the Buddhist disciple and nun Tao-jung—because her conduct in her previous life was not correct—came to be born in her present form, a woman, vile and unclean.

Now if she does not honor the awesome decree of Buddha, how can future consequences be favorable for her? Therefore, having cut down her expenditures on food and clothing, she reverently has had the Nirvana Sutra copied once. She prays that those who read it carefully will be exalted in mind to the highest realms and that those who communicate its meaning will cause others to be so enlightened.

She also prays that in her present existence she will have no further sickness or suffering, that her parents in seven other incarnations (who have already died or will die in the future) and her present family and close relatives may experience joy in the four realms, and that whatever they seek may indeed come to pass. Finally, she prays that all those endowed with knowledge may be included within this prayer.

The lay disciple Madame Tuan (nee Chang) has ever lamented that the fragrant orchid, like a bubble, blooms for but one day, and that separation from loved ones causes so much sorrow. She wonders how it can be that Heaven feels nothing for the calamities it inflicts, and causes the worthiest to be the first to be cut down, just as the young tree is the first to wither and the highest blossoms are the first to fall.

Thus, on behalf of her deceased third son, Commissioner Tuan, an officer of the local commandery, she has reverently had this section of the Golden Light Sutra copied. Now that the transcription is completed, she prays that her son's spirit may visit the blue heavens, that he may mingle with the immortals, that he may travel in person to the Pure Regions and listen to sutras being recited under the tree. She also prays that he may never pass through the three unhappy states of existence or the eight calamities, but will gather Karma sufficient to enable him to proceed joyfully to the Lotus Palace and the Flowering Throne, that he will never again suffer a short life but enjoy longevity in the Pure Land and may be perpetually reborn only there.

His loving mother, thinking of him, prays that the Karma for both of them may be good and that they may both enjoy the fruits of salvation.

Zen Stories

In Zen Buddhism, disciples received their training from a master who already had experienced enlightenment, or Satori. A Zen master might actually beat his students with a wooden sword to shock them out of their ordinary ways of thought. He knew as well how to illustrate the principles of Zen through surprising actions and speeches. Anecdotes about the great Zen masters are among the cherished texts of this form of Buddhism.

1. Joshu asked the teacher Nansen, "What is the true Way?"
   Nansen answered, "Everyday way is the true Way."
   Joshu asked, "Can I study it?"
   Nansen answered, "The more you study, the further from the Way."
   Joshu asked, "If I don't study it, how can I know it?"
   Nansen answered, "The Way does not belong to things

seen: nor to things unseen. It does not belong to things known: nor to things unknown. Do not seek it, study it, or name it. To find yourself on it, open yourself wide as the sky."

2. A master was asked the question, "What is the Way?" by a curious monk.
"It is right before your eyes," said the master.
"Why do I not see it for myself?"
"Because you are thinking of yourself."
"What about you: do you see it?"
"So long as you see double, saying 'I don't', and 'you do,' and so on, your eyes are clouded," said the master.
"When there is neither 'I' nor 'You,' can one see it?"
"When there is neither 'I' nor 'You,' who is the one that wants to see it?"

3. One of the Japanese emperors had given up his throne to follow the way of Buddha. He approached Gudo, a famous master, and asked: "What happens to the man of enlightenment after death?"
Gudo replied, "How should I know?"
"Why, because you're a master," said the ex-emperor.
"Yes," said Gudo, "but not a dead one."

The Tibetan Book of the Dead

An important ritual in Tibetan Buddhism takes place when a person is dying. In the Vajravana tradition, after death a person enters a forty-nine day intermediary state (bardo) between the end of one life and the beginning of another. At this time, a person who is properly prepared can attain Nirvana. If that does not happen, he will remain on the cycle of rebirth.

The Book of the Dead is a spiritual manual that assists the lamas in preparing the dying person to seize this important chance to end the cycle. Different texts of the manual exist. The following are excerpts from one translation.

(The Lama speaks to the dying person): I now transmit to you the profound teaching which I have myself received from my Teacher....Pay attention to it now, and do not allow yourself to be distracted by other thoughts!...If you suffer, do not give in to the pain!....

The factors which made up the person known as (the name of the dying person) are about to disperse. Your mental activities are separating themselves from your body, and they are about to enter the intermediary state. Rouse your energy, so that you may enter this state self-possessed and in full consciousness!

First of all there will appear to you, swifter than lightning, the luminous splendor of the colorless light of Emptiness, and that will surround you on all sides. Terrified, you will want to flee from the radiance....Try to submerge yourself in that light, giving up all belief in a separate self, all attachment to your illusory ego....

If you miss salvation at that moment, you will be forced to have a number of further dreams, both pleasant and unpleasant. Even they offer you a chance to gain understanding....But you must know that all you perceive is a mere vision, a mere illusion, and does not reflect any really existing objects. Have no fear, and form no attachment!...

Three and a half days after your death, Buddhas and Bodhisattvas will for seven days appear to you....Wonderful and delightful though they are, the Buddhas may nevertheless frighten you. Do not give in to your fright! Do not run away!...Pray to them with intense faith and humility, and, in a halo of rainbow light, you will merge into the heart of the divine Father-Mother, and take up your abode in one of the realms of the Buddhas.

CHAPTER 6

The Arts
and Buddhism

*F*rom Afghanistan to Japan, from India to Indonesia, Buddhism has been a major influence on Asian art. Buddhism interacted with many national traditions to produce art works and architecture of incredible variety. The richly gilded temples of Rangoon and Pagan in Myanmar (formerly Burma) represent one ideal. The unfinished wood and simplicity of a Japanese Zen monastery represent another. This chapter will present only a small sample of the Buddhist artistic heritage.

In the earliest Buddhist art, the figure of the Buddha was not shown. "On the dissolution of the body beyond the end of his life," reads a Buddhist text, "neither gods nor men shall know him." The historical Buddha, after his Parinirvana, had passed into invisibility; thus it would have been inappropriate to create his human image. Instead the Buddha was indicated only by symbols—the Bo tree, an empty throne, footprints of the Buddha, a wheel, or a riderless horse.

By the beginning of the common era, that artistic convention began to change. In the centuries since, the image of Buddha has played as important a role in Asian art as Christ did in the art of

Europe. Asian artists worked to express the qualities of enlightenment in physical form. Buddhism provided a stimulus for art of the highest spritual order.

The Image of the Buddha

The first image of the Buddha appears on a coin struck by King Kanishka. The coin-image shows a standing Buddha dressed in a monastic robe. A halo surrounds his head and he has a topknot of hair and elongated earlobes. One hand is raised in a blessing.

Kanishka's empire was the birthplace of sculpture depicting the Buddha. There were two different styles. In Gandhara in the northern part of the empire, the style reflected the Greco-Roman heritage. Buddha was dressed in robes that were draped in Greek fashion. His head was sculpted with wavy hair.

Another style, influenced by Hindu art, appeared in Mathura in the south. The Mathura Buddhas were clothed in a light Indian dhoti, or long skirt. The hair was straight and tied in a topknot. Molded out of sandstone, these images were closer to Indian sculpture styles, with soft, gentle curves. The Buddha is smiling gently. From these two traditions, the classical Buddhist image arose. It has certain characteristics that make it immediately recognizable, in spite of different national and ethnic traditions.

In general, the Buddha-image is smiling. The smile of the Buddha suggests an experience of unearthly beauty. It represents

Preceding page-Interior of Sokkuram Grotto. Feel the serenity and peace in this chaitya hall, created not only by the Buddha's iconographical image but also by the artistic and architectural style within which the image is enshrined.

Symbolic representations of the Buddha: Footprints, Bo Tree, Riderless Horse, and Wheel

an ideal of calm and inner peace. Often the eyes are closed, but the Buddha is not sleeping—he is looking within.

Many times, the Buddha is shown sitting on a lotus throne. The lotus plant has a deep symbolic significance in Buddhism. The roots of the plant are embedded in the mud under water, but the flower blooms above the water. Just so, the Buddha lived in a corrupt world, but kept his purity.

The Buddha's holiness is also indicated by marks called lakshanas. It was believed that the Buddha had thirty-two lakshanas, which were signs that he was an enlightened one. The one most often seen in his portrayals is the halo that surrounds either his head or whole body. Called the prabhamandala, it indicates his divinity. The topknot or protuberance (the ushanisha) on top of his head signifies the super brain with the supreme wisdom that Buddha attained at his Enlightenment. The long earlobes indicate that as a prince, Buddha wore heavy gold and precious-stone earrings; thus they are a reminder of the Buddha's renunciation of material things. Finally, the urna, or mark on the forehead, is a sign of spiritual insight. On some statues, the urna may be inset with a precious stone.

The Buddha figure was portrayed in various positions, or asanas, appropriate for teaching, blessing, or meditation. His hand gestures (mudras) were also conventionalized. The right hand held palm outward with the fingers pointing upward is a teaching gesture. The hand position signifying deep meditation shows the hands on the lap, palms up, with the right hand over the left.

Images of the Buddha spread beyond India. In China, the earliest Buddhist art was influenced by the Gandhara style. These Buddhas were done in gilt bronze with heavy concentric folds in the robes. Instead of the traditional semi-nudity of Indian gods and goddesses, Chinese sculptures were covered by scarves, shawls and skirts. In time, the image of the Buddha took on a distinctly Chinese appearance.

■ *Top—***Abhaya Mudra**—*The gesture of Reassurance*
*Middle—***Dharma Chakra Mudra**—*The gesture of teaching the Middle Way*
*Bottom—***Dhyana Mudra**—*The gesture of meditation*

The Korean Buddha at Sokkuram Grotto, on Mt. Toham, is one of the great achievements of Asian art. Carved entirely from the rock face of the mountain, a towering Buddha gazes outward toward the sea. The Buddha is seated in the Pose of Enlightenment. His legs are folded in the "lotus postion," the left hand lies palm up in the lap, and the right hand rests palm down on the right knee. The morning sun glints off a jeweled urna on his forehead. The pose was designed to create a spiritual experience in the viewer.

At Bamiyan in Afghanistan, a mammoth Buddha was carved out of a huge cliff. This was the Buddha Vairocana, the cosmic and omnipresent Buddha. The statue's immense size indicated his role as savior of the world. In 2001, the Taliban rulers of Afghanistan ordered the destruction of the statue, one of Afghanistan's pre-Islamic treasures. Countries around the world protested the order, but the statue was reduced to rubble. A priceless part of Afghanistan's Buddhist history was lost forever.

Another Buddha Vairocana was created in Nara, Japan. In the eighth century, the Japanese emperor asked for contributions for this Buddha to fulfill a vow made when an epidemic of smallpox swept the country. The casting of the bronze image was an enormous task. Fifty-three feet high and weighing over 200 tons, it was gilded with 500 pounds of gold. Taking pride and joy in their achievement, the Japanese dedicated the statue in the Todaiji Temple in 752, exactly two hundred years after Japan received its first image from Korea. At the dedicatory ceremony—called the "eye-opening"—the Great Buddha was presented to the people in the grandest celebration Japan had ever seen.

The Reclining Buddha of Sri Lanka is also of enormous size. This position represents the Buddha's death, or Parinirvana. Unique to Thailand are walking Buddhas, some with undulating arms that represent another of the Buddha's asanas, the resemblance of his limbs to the trunk of an elephant.

Whatever the pose, the Buddha-figure has brought out the best in Asian artists. Most of these works were done by anonymous Buddhist monks, whose sculpting was an act of devotion. The growing pantheon of bodhisattvas and buddhas of the past and future heightened the inspiration for the art.

The Importance of the Stupa

Buddhist architecture started very simply with the stupa. A stupa is a mound-shaped structure, first used to cover the ashes and relics of the Buddha. The early stupas were constructed of

■ *The time-worn Buddhas of Bamiyan Province were among Afghanistan's most precious pre-Islamic treasures. They were destroyed by the Taliban in 2001.*

mud bricks and subject to disintegration. In appearance these structures were simple and uninspiring. Still, the stupa remained the basic architectural design of Buddhist temples. As a circular structure, it appropriately resembled—in three-dimensional form—the wheel of the Dharma.

Over time, stupas became more elaborate. The mound that held the relic increased in size. Its summit was often flattened, with the top enclosed by a railing. This high place represented the heaven of the gods who governed the visible world. Frequently an umbrella (or a series of umbrellas) rose above it, symbolic of royal power—the power of the Buddha and his Dharma.

The most important early stupa is at Sanchi in Central India. The Buddha never visited Sanchi, but Asoka did. It was the site of the monastery from which Asoka sent Mahinda to Sri Lanka to convert that country to Buddhism. Asoka's wife, Devi, founded

■ The central dome of the great stupa at Sanchi. Here Buddha's remains were buried by King Ashoka about 2,300 years ago. Notice the three-tiered umbrella at the dome's summit, symbolizing Buddha, Dharma, and Sangha.

the monastery, and her husband later started the stupa to commemorate his bringing of the Dharma to Sri Lanka. The original stupa measured about sixty feet in diameter and about twenty-five feet in height.

Over time, the Sanchi stupa was doubled in size and its older wooden railings were replaced with massive nine-feet-high stone balustrades. (These are today covered with the names of pilgrims who have visited over the centuries.)

To strengthen the dome of the stupa, it was covered with stone blocks and topped with a three-tiered umbrella. The three levels of the umbrella represented the Three Jewels of Buddhism: the Teacher (Buddha), the Law (Dharma) and the community of monks (Sangha). Four magnificently carved gateways, each thirty-four feet high, faced the four points of the compass. The square columns depict various events from the life of the Buddha and his previous lives—a sculptured representation of the Jataka.

By the fifth century C.E., the early brick dome of the Sanchi stupa was completely transformed into a "world mountain." At the base of the stupa sat four images of the Buddha, facing each of the gates. The tiered umbrella symbolically joins the heaven with the earth through the huge dome.

No one could enter the stupa itself, for it was completely sealed. The stupa was not a place to house worshipers, but an enclosure for the relic. Traditionally, Buddhists paid homage at holy sites by walking around them (circumnambulation). At Sanchi, a stone walkway was built around the stupa at a height of sixteen feet above the ground. A staircase enabled worshipers to reach it.

The largest stupa in the world is on the island of Java in Indonesia. Java was visited by traders and missionaries and settled by Indian colonizers, who brought to the island both Hinduism and Buddhism. In the eighth century, Java became the center of a seagoing empire governed by the Sailendra (King of the Mountain) Dynasty. The Sailendra kings were ardent Buddhists, and under their patronage the island experienced a flowering of culture. The greatest achievement of the Sailendras was the Borobodur, whose name means "Monastery of Accumulated Virtue."

The giant stupa at Borobodur symbolizes the Mahayana Buddhist view of the universe and consists of six square terraces surmounted by three circular terraces. The stupa is symbolic of the Mahayana Buddhist view of the universe. At the lower levels, sculpted reliefs show humans bound to the cycle of rebirth. Higher up are beautiful scenes from the life of Siddhartha Gautama. Various bodhisattvas are also portrayed. Carved in the upper circular terraces are images of the Buddha in contemplation. At the very top is a huge, undecorated stupa. It represents the eternally unseen and unseeing—the Void, or Nirvana. The entire stupa shows in stone the path humankind can follow to reach Nirvana, according to the Mahayana view. Each year, Buddhist pilgrims come to the shrine to honor the three most important events in the Buddha's life—his birth, enlightenment, and death. Touching the Buddha figures is believed to bring good luck.

In China, the stupa evolved into the pagoda, a tall, multistoried tower. Chinese pagodas are octagonal in shape and always have an odd number of stories, ranging from three to thirteen. Like the Indian stupas, they enclose Buddhist relics. After Buddhism was accepted in China, pagodas sprang up throughout the country. They were built of wood, however, and few survive. One, the Big Goose Pagoda, remains standing in the former Chinese capital of Changan (today's Sian).

The spread of Buddhism from China to Korea, Vietnam, and Japan brought with it the multi-storied pagoda architectural style. By the seventh century C.E., pagodas were found in all three countries. They were often part of complexes that included study centers and a building, or hall, for worship. The worship hall must have fostered a sense of religious feeling. Usually it had an enormous roof over its high, spacious interior. Yet the light was not too bright, so that one had the proper sense of awe for the large image of the deity. Outside, leading to the worship hall, was a ceremonial gateway decorated with images of the guardian deities of Mahayana Buddhism.

In Myanmar (Burma), the top of the stupa became elongated into a distinctive spire. One of the most beautiful examples is the Shwe Dagon temple at Rangoon. The temple contains eight sacred hairs of the Buddha.

■ *Five Stories Pagoda in Horuji Temple in Nara, Japan*

Building pagodas took on a unique urgency in Burma. After King Arawrahta seized the Buddhist scriptures from the Mon city of Thaton around 1060, he brought them back to his capital, Pagan, in jeweled cases on white elephants. He started building pagodas to demonstrate his religious piety. The laity, rich and poor alike, were inspired to join the effort so they could gain spiritual merit, or good Karma.

From the year 1044 to about 1300, Burma's kings and commoners went on a frenzy of building. An eleventh-century stone dedication tablet describes a king who paid six oxcarts of silver for artisans to build a pagoda in his name. Kings were demanding in their standards. One threatened to execute a bricklayer if a needle could be inserted between the bricks of the pagoda. Price was no object, for Pagan became prosperous through trade with India and Sri Lanka.

During this 250-year period, five thousand pagodas were built, creating a veritable forest of towers on the plain where the city stands. The total works out to about two pagodas each month. All were different—some ornate, some simple, large and small. Many were lavishly decorated with wall paintings and sculptures. Pagan's enormous effort is unprecedented in history.

The frantic construction came to an end when the Mongol chief, Kublai Khan, defeated the Burmese in battle. Pagan never regained its former political greatness. Over time, many of the pagodas deteriorated or were destroyed. Even so, about two thousand remain today, a ghostly reflection of the city's past greatness.

Monastery Complexes

At the same time that stupas and pagodas were spreading through Asia, developments were taking place in another kind of building: the Buddhist monastery. This stucture consisted of prayer halls (chaityas) and living quarters (Viharas) with individual cells for the monks.

Sometimes these halls and chambers were not built of wood or stone, but hewn out of large rock formations. Rock-hewn architecture appealed to the Buddhist monks for several reasons. First, it was durable and stable. Second, such a dwelling continued the tradition of hermits and ascetics living in caves. Third, the cave-mountains were located in secluded areas. The carved mountain became the perfect sanctuary for Buddhist monks.

Some of these stone-hewn constructions grew to an immense size. Looking at these giant architecture-sculptures today, the visitor is amazed to realize that they were excavated by monks who carved the cliff face away inch by inch. First an overall plan was devised. Then the sculptors carved the facade by cutting a rough opening which ultimately became the finished ceiling. This permitted them to work back and down through hundreds of square yards of solid stone and eventually to the chamber floor. The unwanted rock was removed, and then the rock still embedded in the earth was shaped into rough forms by using iron picks. Finally, the finishing was done with hand chisels.

A physical stone stupa was placed within the chaitya hall. The layout of the chaitya hall is a long chamber divided by two rows of columns. In a rounded end or apse, the two aisles meet and curve around the stupa which holds relics and treasures of the monastery.

The viharyas, or monks' quarters, were generally designed as open square halls approached by a doorway through a porch. The doorway was encircled by small cells for the monks carved deeper into the rock. Here members of the Sangha lived, meditated, and slept in close proximity to their prayer hall and the stupa. As the priestly community increased, more cells were excavated farther away.

In the course of time, small study-rooms were added. Eventually a complex monastery was created. It consisted of the common room, a refectory, a kitchen, a tank for the water supply, and cells. The monasteries were centers of Buddhist learning and great Buddhist art.

The cave monasteries were particularly noted for their wall murals. The greatest of the Indian murals are at Ajanta, in the southern region of India known as the Decca. Located on a high bluff near the town of Aurangabad, the caves sheltered monks as early as 200 B.C.E. Thirty caves have been discovered. Five of them are chaityas, or chapels for worship, and the rest Viharas where the monks lived. The site was abandoned by the year 650 C.E. and not rediscovered until 1819.

The glorious Ajanta murals were inspired by both major traditions of Buddhism—Mahayana and Theraveda. From floor to ceiling the walls swirl with color and form. The stone was prepared by applying a series of surfaces, ending with a thin coat of white plaster. After the paint was put down, the murals were polished to give them a luster that the centuries have only slightly diminished. Even in the dim light, the Ajanta paintings shine with strong, vivid colors.

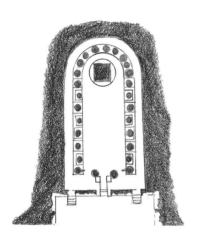

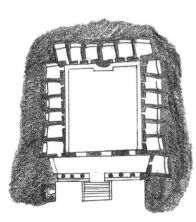

■ *Top–Plan of an assembly hall,* **Chaitya,** *with a* **Stupa** *Bottom–Plan of a monastery,* **Vihara**

■ *Chaitya hall, showing an interior stupa with Buddha's image carved on its outer wall*

The subject matter is a breathtaking record of the Buddha's life and teachings. One immense painting of the reclining Buddha, preparing for his Parinirvana, is angled to catch the sun from the mouth of the cave. The moving shadows play across the Buddha's face, which seems to change expression in the light.

The caves also display scenes from the Jataka Tales. Other legends are illustrated, such as the temptation of the Buddha by the beautiful daughters of Mara, and the legendary incident when the Buddha, taunted by an unbeliever, took the shape of a thousand Buddhas to convince him of his divinity.

In addition, the artists depicted scenes from royal and upper-class Indian life—probably to commemorate the patrons who sponsored the Sangha that flourished in these caves. Scholars have found these to be a treasure-trove of information about Indian life of the period.

Similarly, the largest surviving source of early Chinese painting is at Tun Huang, the Caves of the Thousand Buddhas. The walls contain pictures of all stages of the Buddha's life. All the favorite buddhas and bodhisattvas of the Chinese Mahayana faith are included. Artists here also portrayed vivid images of the different heavens on the way to Nirvana. Even Hsuan-tsang appears in scenes that show the hardships of his pilgrimage to India.

Tibetan Arts

The art of Tibet is almost entirely religious, used for the ceremonies and traditions of Tantric Buddhism. The most common form of art is the painted banner (tanka). The tankas are hung in temples and at family altars; they are carried by lamas in processions and used to illustrate sermons. Besides the Buddha, the subject matter of the tankas includes other buddhas, bodhisattvas and famous lamas. The Buddha often holds a thunderbolt, symbolic of the Tantric tradition, or a bell, which symbolizes the Void.

Another tradition of Tibetan painting is the mandala, a geometric figure—usually a circle inside a square—that is regarded as the "dwelling of the god." The object itself is used to gain supernatural powers. At the center is a figure of the Buddha or some other divinity. Surrounding it are fantastically intricate symbols and depictions of other gods and religious scenes. By meditating on the mandala, a person can attain unity with the divine element. Some mandalas are constructed in sand or even butter for specific ceremonies, after which they are destroyed.

Tibetan sculpture also uses butter, as well as precious metals and other more permanent substances. Huge images are placed in the temples, and smaller ones on family shrines. The devout carry miniature images with them as "pocket-shrines." Whatever

■ *A Buddhist diagram of the Cosmic Lotus used for meditation (Tibet)*

the size of the image, it contains a cavity in the back that is filled with rolls of prayers or sacred relics. These are placed within the figure at a ceremony conducted by a lama. (The contents are sometimes called "sacred intestines.")

Tibetan art has also produced numerous ritual objects, the most famous of which is the prayer wheel. This is a round metal case or cylinder which revolves on a stick. Mantras, or prayers, are either engraved on the cylinder or placed inside on paper. By turning the cylinder, a person can gain the same merit he would earn by reciting the mantra—except, of course, the cylinder can be rotated more quickly than reciting the words aloud.

Zen Arts

Zen Buddhism had a very important influence on Japanese arts, which took on many of the aspects of the sect itself. Zen arts share the values of simplicity, austerity, purity, and an emphasis on the calm that comes from meditation. One can see this in the typical Japanese Buddhist monastery. It is constructed of plain unfinished wood with white washed plaster. There is no sculpture, for worship of the Buddha has been deemphasized. The whole panoply of Mahayana Buddhist figures is absent. At the center of the monastery is the meditation hall. The library, such an important part of other sects' monasteries, is less important, for the Buddhist scriptures also have been deemphasized. The architecture is simple and functional.

One unique Japanese form that arose in the thirteenth century was the tea ceremony. By tradition, Eisai, who brought Rinzai Zen to Japan from China, also brought tea. He advocated tea drinking for health and to keep oneself alert during meditation. Over time an elaborate tea ritual developed, in which each movement in preparing, serving, and drinking tea is rigidly prescribed.

In a simple wood building, the participants enter through a low door. By this act they humble themselves. Within there is little furniture or decoration, except a beautiful object (such as a flower or tree sprig) in an alcove and a low table around which the participants are served tea. The tea and the utensils in which it is brewed and served are spare and simple. Each action, from the pouring of boiling water to the drinking, is choreographed. It is believed that the simple, ritualized movements help the participants to cleanse their minds for contemplation.

Zen also affected Japanese painting. In keeping with the deemphasis of the Mahayana hierarchy of buddhas and bodhisattvas, there were no religious scenes. Instead Zen painters produced portraits of Zen masters. These simple, realistic, and psychologically acute portraits are among the greatest ever produced.

However, Zen ideas influenced secular as well as religious art. Most importantly, the Doctrine of Emptiness (the Void) inspired artists to "show by what is not shown." Japanese painters do not fill canvases or paper with brush-strokes. Much of the space occupied by the painting is empty—at least to the eye. The mind fills it in with what the artists has suggested.

Zen infused the painting style known as sumi-e. Artists used only black ink and a brush to produce subtle shades from light grey to black. Often the picture consisted of little more than swirls—which, however, suggested much more. "It takes only one blade of grass to show the wind's direction" was a Japanese saying.

Other artists used the "flung-ink" style to give the art a feeling of spontaneity. The goal was to grasp the inner spirit of the subject, creating a world of suggestion, rather than explicit forms.

Zen also influenced gardens. The Japanese had been influenced by the Chinese view of a garden as a world in miniature. The essential elements of Chinese gardens were rocks (implying mountains), water, and plants. The Japanese took this a step further by simplifying the elements even more. The most famous garden in the world is at Ryoanji Temple in Kyoto. It contains no living thing. Fifteen carefully placed rocks rest on white raked sand. This abstract design is a garden that involves the mind and invites meditation.

Although the No, or Noh, theater uses many elements of ancient Japanese drama, it strives for a Zen goal. Its objective is to portray meanings that go beyond words. In slow movements that resemble a dance, the masked actors tell stories of universal appeal. But in true Zen fashion, No drama teaches more through intuition than statement. The test of judgment for a No performance is whether it possesses "the true flower."

"The true flower" is a reference to Siddartha Gautama himself. A story about the Buddha tells of an occasion when he was seated around pilgrims who had come to hear him preach the law. The Buddha held up a flower in silence. The crowd was mystified except for Kashpaya who looked at the flower and smiled inwardly. Buddha saw that he had understood "that which goes beyond the word." Kashyapa became the first of the twenty-eight Great Patriarchs—the last being Bodhidharma, who brought the Meditation School from India.

CHAPTER *7*

The Year
in Buddhism

*A*s midnight approaches on the last day of the year, men, women, and children gather at the Buddhist temple of Chion-in. Here, in the ancient Japanese city of Kyoto, monks prepare for the ceremonies that will usher in the New Year. Exactly at midnight, a group takes hold of a huge log and strikes the end of it against a bell. The deep sound reverberates throughout the city again and again. At each of the 108 strokes of the bell, the monks recite one of the frailties of humankind.

Children come forward with strands of rope, lighting one end at the temple flame. They will take the burning ropes home to rekindle the kitchen fire and light the candles at the household shrines. This is the day for beginning again, a time of hope and renewal.

Traditionally, in the days before New Year's, people have paid their debts, cleaned house, bought new clothes, and exchanged gifts to start the year with a clean slate. The ceremonies are tied to the Buddhist ideas of rebirth and purification.

Though the New Year begins on different days of the year in Buddhist countries with lunar calendars (based on the moon's

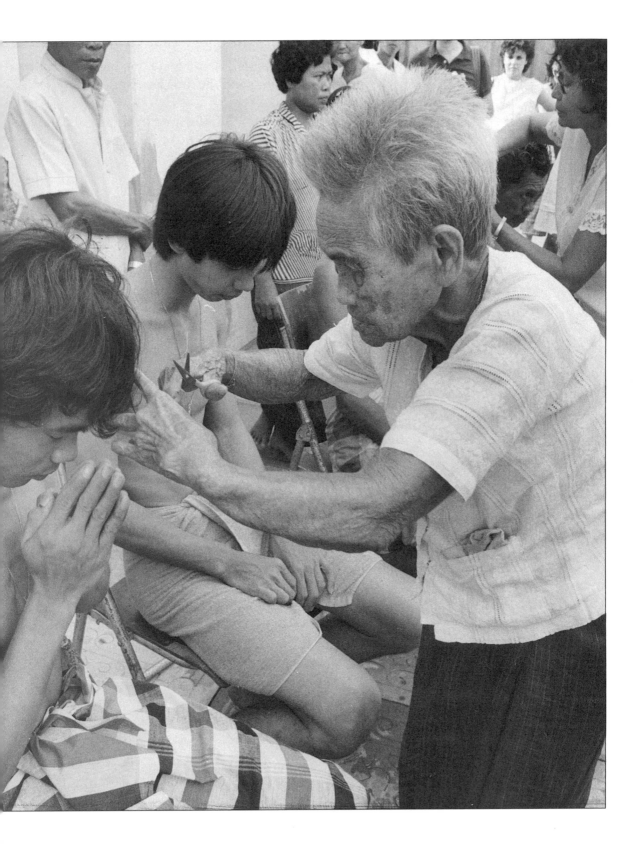

■ Preceding page-
A grandmother begins the
ordination ceremony for
initiate monks by cutting
the first locks of her
grandson's hair.

phases), people everywhere mark it in their own fashion. Frequently the New Year Day is a nationwide holiday in which no work is done, and people spend the time feasting, dancing, singing, and playing games.

Each form of celebration is influenced by local and national customs. The open and flexible spirit of the Buddhist religion embraces many forms of worship and ritual.

Rites of Passage

The practice of Buddhism does not, strictly speaking, require a temple or the intercession of a monk. Anyone can follow the teachings of Buddhism in his or her daily life. The temples provide a refuge for those who wish to devote themselves more deeply to the teachings of the Buddha. Members of the Sangha, however, are frequently called on to participate in ceremonies marking important events in people's lives—birth, marriage, and death.

Customs vary from country to country. In most Theravada countries, when a child is born, its parents take it to the local temple to be given a name. The baby is blessed by the monks and sprinkled with holy water. A wax candle is lit and tilted on its side so that the drops of molten wax fall into a bowl of water. This ceremony symbolizes the coming together of the four elements: earth, air, fire, and water.

At some Theravada marriage ceremonies, the young man and woman go to the local temple with their friends and relations. A long cotton thread is wound around the image of the Buddha and then around all those present. Symbolically united in one community, the congregation chants hymns and the chief monk gives his blessing. Then the monk cuts two pieces from the thread and winds one around the wrist of the groom. The groom winds the other around his bride's wrist—for monks are not supposed to touch women. However, in some Buddhist countries, monks do not attend weddings, for it is regarded as bad luck.

Monks have a special role at Buddhist funerals. When a member of a household dies, a monk is summoned to recite special sermons and the sutra of the dead. In Mahayana countries such as China, Taiwan, and Korea, where special veneration is commonly paid to ancestors, the monk makes a tablet for the newly dead person to be placed on the family altar.

The monk applies the "last water" to the lips of the dead body, after which the body is bathed and properly dressed. A funeral ceremony follows. The friends and neighbors of the deceased show their sympathy by offering "incense money." The incense is burned at the cremation and the mourners may speak to honor and remember the deceased. After the funeral, the family hosts a vegetarian dinner.

Death rites commonly continue for a number of days, during which the bereaved family invites monks to eat in their household. This is done in order to transfer merit to the dead person, in case he or she has not accumulated enough good Karma. Some families commemorate the death at another meal three months later, and on the first year's anniversary of the death.

Religious Observances

Buddhists are not required to attend regular services at a temple, as Christians do on Sunday or Jews on Saturday. Nor do Buddhists have specified daily times of prayer as Muslims do. However, in Theravada Buddhism, devout laypeople may observe a "sabbath" called the uposatha. This falls on the 1st, 8th, 15th, and 23rd days of the lunar month. The faithful bring offerings to the temple on these days. Some may observe the day by remaining in seclusion to meditate, and use the temple for this purpose. Others may listen to religious sermons. On these days, the monks at the temple usually organize special rites that can include music, processions, and even fireworks displays.

During the monsoon season that comes at differing times from June to October in Southeast Asia, Buddhists observe a time of penitence that is the equivalent of Christian Lent. During the approximately three-month season, monks observe stricter religious duties. Lay people increase their donations to the Sangha and accumulate merit by meditating and listening to sutras.

This tradition may be the oldest one of the religion. For it dates from the time when the Buddha himself, along with his disciples, wandered through northeastern India preaching the

Dharma. The rainy season, which in the nations of Southeast Asia is severe, required that the Buddha and his followers seek a place of refuge while it lasted.

The end of the penitential season is celebrated in special ways. The Buddhists of Burma, for example, celebrate the three-day Festival of Thadingyut (Lights). This commemorates the Buddha's return to earth (after reaching Nirvana), accompanied by angels. Burmese villages and towns are decorated with oil lamps, candles, and electric lights that burn all night long. Balloons bearing flames are sent aloft, and the streets are filled with processions and dancing.

The monsoon season is also the time for another important religous observance, called the vassa, or rain-retreat. This is the time when young people may choose to enter the Sangha. In most Buddhist countries every boy over the age of seven is supposed to enter the Sangha at least temporarily. He lives in the monastery for about two weeks for a vigorous religious training. In some countries, it is also common for adult males to enter the Sangha temporarily at this time, to accumulate merit for themselves.

Festivals Celebrating Buddhism

In many Buddhist countries, events in the life of the Buddha are commemorated at different times of the year. On these days, people visit a temple, bringing offerings of incense, cloth, flowers, and money. Often, more elaborate celebrations involve everyone in the local community, much as Christmas is celebrated in predominately Christian countries.

In Laos, the Buddha's birthday is part of the New Year's Celebration. Holy water is poured on the statues of Buddha, and as part of the festivities, people drench each other with buckets of water in the streets. Caged birds are set free, and live fish are returned to the rivers.

In Japan, the Japanese Buddhists celebrate Hana Matsuri, the Buddha's birthday, on April 8. Traditionally, people pour tea over the images of Buddha in temples and homes. Special Zen holidays also occur at different times of the year. Some of these, such as Bodhidharma Day, commemorate important figures in the history of Zen.

A very popular Japanese holiday is the Feast of O-Bon. On this day, by tradition, the souls of the dead come to mingle with the living. People invite their neighbors and friends for an all-night feast. At dawn, the living place little paper boats—holding candles, fruit, and flowers—in a nearby stream or lake. The boats carry off the souls of the dead.

The ceremony stems from a Buddhist story that is much beloved in Japan. A young man named Mokuren had a dream of his mother in Gaki, the Hell of Starvation. Spirits were punished there by having lavish feasts set before them, but when the spirits raised the food to their mouths, it turned into flames.

Mokuren, the story goes, asked the Buddha how to redeem his mother from this torment. The Buddha advised him to practice purity and kindness and to study the sutras. Mokuren became a bhikku, and after many years dreamed that he had accumulated enough merit to set his mother free. In gratitude, he set out a wondrous feast for the villagers. This was the first Feast of O-Bon.

In Theravada countries, the birth, enlightenment, and Parinirvana of the Buddha are believed to have occurred on the same day (in different years). Called by various names, such as, Vaishaklia Puja in India, Visakha Buja in Laos, Balsakh Purnima in Nepal, and Wesak in Sri Lanka, this triple celebration occurs on the day of the full moon in May. Colorful religious processions wind around the temple three times and then move through the streets beyond the temple. Plays depicting the events of the Buddha's life are presented.

One of the most colorful Buddhist celebrations takes place in Kandy, a city in Sri Lanka. The Temple of the Tooth in Kandy houses the most precious of Sri Lankan Buddhist relics—a tooth of the Buddha that was found after his cremation. The relic is enclosed within seven jeweled caskets that are never opened. However, in August, on the feast of Esala Perahera, a replica of the innermost casket is carried through the torchlit streets on the back of a magnificently caparisoned elephant. Crowds of pilgrims come for the occasion.

In the Himalayan kingdom of Sikkim, where the Tantric form of Buddhism is dominant, a joyful and colorful celebration

■ *An elaborate Buddhist "Tooth Relic" procession in Kandy, Sri Lanka. This procession usually takes place once a year.*

takes place in May. This is the anniversary of Padmasambhava's arrival in Tibet with the Dharma. Brightly costumed "demons" gather in the streets, once more trying to chase Padmasambhava away. A lama wearing a fierce-looking mask takes the role of Padmasambhava, and uses his magical techniques to vanquish the demons. Leading the triumphal procession are lamas wearing semi-circular yellow hats that are also a badge of authority in Tibet, Mongolia, and Nepal.

Life Within the Sangha

From the first, the Sangha—the orders of monks and nuns—have occupied a special place in Buddhism. While the Buddha was alive, he established the Sangha so that people could devote themselves fully to his Middle Way.

In the Theravada community, the only way for devout members to attain Nirvana is to enter the Sangha. For only through the monastic life can one completely follow the Eightfold Path. For that reason, it is common to place young boys in a monastery. At the age of eight, they can receive a lower form of ordination, called "The Going Forth." The child is dressed in his best clothes and carried to the monastery by his father; friends and relatives join the procession.

At the door, in imitation of the Buddha, the child casts off his clothing and receives the yellow robe. His head is shaved and he is given the begging bowl and the other possessions of a monk. As a novice, he will be placed in the care of two monks. One will be his companion, the other his teacher. The novice prostrates himself before the companion and announces his intention to take refuge in the Buddha, the Dharma, and the Sangha.

■ If a person when young and strong does not arise and strive when he should arise and strive, and thus sinks into laziness and lack of determination; he will never find the path of wisdom.
From the **Dhammapada** (20:280)

■ Two young novice monks on their daily rounds. The monk in the foreground holds lotus flowers—the quintessential Buddhist symbol of purity.

Novices are taught ten precepts, or rules. They are:
1. To refrain from taking life
2. To refrain from stealing
3. To refrain from sexual activity
4. To refrain from lying
5. To refrain from intoxicating substances
6. To refrain from eating after midday
7. To refrain from the use of perfumes and personal adornment
8. To refrain from seeing public entertainment
9. To refrain from grand beds
10. To refrain from accepting gold or silver.

The young novices are also taught the two cardinal virtues of wisdom and compassion, and that nothing should be believed just because it is a tradition or it is said by a teacher. A novice who chooses to stay will receive a final ordination at the age of twenty. The Buddhist ordination ceremony is formal and impressive. It can only be performed by a group of at least ten monks. The novice must request ordination three times, giving the name of his teacher and requesting anyone who opposes his ordination to speak. He receives a new name and three garments, including an outer and an inner robe as well as a cloak. Thereafter, he must follow a stricter code of more than 220 rules, called the Pratimoksa.

The procedure and ceremonies for becoming a Buddhist nun are much the same. If the novice is under age twenty or has been married for more than twelve years, she must serve a probationary period of two years. The nuns' garments include a skirt and a belt. The nuns are also governed by regulations that make them subordinate to the monks. For example, every two weeks nuns must go to the community of monks to receive instruction, but they can neither instruct nor admonish a monk.

A typical large monastery includes a Monks' Hall, where the members sleep in individual cells, and a Sangha Hall, where they gather to eat, read aloud the sutras, and conduct meetings about monastery business. There may also be an Inner Hall, where images of the Buddha and bodhisattvas are erected as an aid to meditation. Monasteries also include large libraries, where the

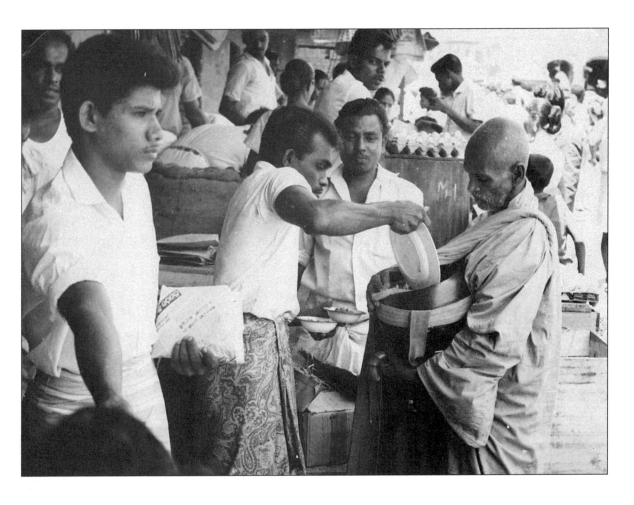

many texts and scriptures of the religion are stored. Finally, there is a Dharma Hall, where monks preach to the laity.

The traditional life of the monastery is intended to provide a suitable setting for monks and nuns to pursue the goal of enlightenment. The members of the Sangha rise very early and devote themselves to meditation. At the appropriate time, they dress to go out with their wooden bowls to beg for food or other offerings. They chant hymns or ring a gong to attract attention to their begging.

Returning to the monastery, they wash their feet and a little before noon eat their only meal of the day. In the afternoon, older monks give instruction to the younger ones, and then return to

■ This picture shows a lay person offering alms to a Buddhist monk in Sri Lanka. In Buddhism, one way of gaining merit is to offer meals to monks on their daily rounds. Offering meals is a sacred rite and is to be performed in a ritualistic manner.

private meditation. Frequently, in the heat of the day, they seek refuge under a tree to imitate the meditation of the Buddha under the Bo tree.

At sunset, the Dharma Hall is opened to the laity who gather to hear sermons and ask questions. Memorizing, preserving, and teaching the Dharma is the greatest service a monk can perform for others. Some preach in public places or before small gatherings in homes. The laity often place food and flowers before the chair of the Buddhist preacher. By custom, he should not preach until he has been requested three times, but then will teach anyone who sincerely asks. Until recently, especially in Theravada countries, the monks were the sole teachers and preservers of culture.

In the early evening, the monks assemble in the Sangha Hall to read aloud from the scriptures and discuss their own spiritual concerns. Monasteries are not organized as a spiritual hierarchy. Any important decisions must be agreed on unanimously. Nor do the monks pledge obedience, as in Christian monasteries. In practice, however, certain monks are assigned specific duties that involve authority. Some, for example, are in charge of teaching the novices, others supervise the monastery garden, and so forth. A senior monk is usually accepted as the leader of the group.

Twice a month, on the days of the full moon and new moon, comes posadha, or "Observance Day." The senior monk in the Sangha Hall asks the other resident monks to declare openly their faults and misdeeds. Any monk who knows he is guilty and remains silent is committing a voluntary falsehood, violating the rule of the Sangha. Very rarely, and only for specified serious offenses, a monk may be expelled from the Sangha.

In general, the above description applies to most Buddhist monasteries today. However, just as the practice of the religion has developed many different forms, so has the life of the Sangha. Because the laity can gain merit by donating food, cloth, money, and other gifts to the monastery, the daily needs of the monks are provided without the necessity of begging with a bowl. Even so, the practice has survived as a symbol of the monk's withdrawal from ordinary life. Some Sangha communities do not eat flesh or fish; others will accept them if the animal was not killed on their behalf. Monks are also permitted to accept invitations to meals at the homes of the laity.

Stricter traditions also survive, sometimes in protest against the more liberal, wordly customs of the Sangha in urban areas. In Sri Lanka, "forest monks" retreat into the remote areas of the country to live in caves or tents, meditating on the Dharma. They attract pilgrims who make long journeys to give them alms and listen to their sermons.

The Buddhist Sangha has adapted to the modern world. Greater emphasis is given to practical social reform. The laity are encouraged to forego giving alms and instead to support the Sangha's establishment of schools, hospitals, and shelters for the homeless. Buddhist Sanghas have joined international organizations, which meet to discuss contemporary issues such as nuclear disarmament, international justice, and human rights.

CHAPTER 8

Buddhism Today

*A*s we enter the twenty-first century, Buddhists are exploring the ways that their tradition relates to the social, cultural, and political situations in the world around them. They are far more culturally and nationally diverse than ever before. One hundred years ago, Buddhism was still mainly centered in its Asian birthplace. Today it reaches around the world.

In recent years, Buddhists have become more socially engaged. Buddhists work actively with the poor, the homeless, the addicted, the dying, and those in prison. In San Francisco, Buddhists run a major AIDS counseling service. Buddhists in New York teach classes in the Tibetan language and culture to children of Tibetan refugees. In Taiwan, Buddhist organizations build hospitals and contribute to disaster relief. Around the world, Buddhists have become more politically aware. They campaign against nuclear weapons, the arms trade, and the destruction of the environment. Buddhist scholars continue to examine the Buddhist teachings in light of modern-day problems, such as human rights and medical ethics. They work to provide followers with guidelines for living an upright life.

The Buddhist Revival

■ *Preceding page-The Reclining Buddha. Such statues depict Buddha at the time of **Parinirvana**, the passing from the phenomenal world. In Buddhist thought, death is simply the dispersement of the five **Skhandas**, not the end of life.*

In the sixteenth century, the first European traders arrived in Sri Lanka. With their arrival, Buddhist countries encountered European culture. Europeans soon colonized countries such as Sri Lanka, Burma, Laos, Cambodia, and Vietnam. Christian missionaries followed and began to gain converts. Where Theravada Buddhism had once flourished, the religion faltered.

In the nineteenth century, a growing sense of nationalism began to sweep through southern Asia. In many countries,

■ *The 150-foot-high Malabodhi Temple in Bodh Gaya stands in the place where Buddha attained Enlightenment. The original shrine was built during Asoka's reign.*

nationalism led to a strengthening of Buddhism. The Buddhist revival began in Siam (now Thailand), which Europeans had never colonized. King Rama IV (r. 1851–1868) had been a Buddhist monk before becoming king. He instigated reforms in the Sangha and began to modernize his country. Similar efforts were taking place elsewhere. In Burma (now Myanmar), King Mindon (r. 1853–1878) made Buddhist revival a goal. In Sri Lanka in 1873, Buddhists invited a Methodist minister and a Buddhist monk to debate the merits of the two religions. The Buddhist won, and newspapers around the world reported the event, creating new enthusiasm for the Buddhist faith. In 1892, Anagarike Dharmapala, a Sri Lankan, founded the first international Buddhist organization, the Bodh Gaya Society. One of its goals was to unite all Buddhists.

The efforts to revitalize the Sangha in southern Asia were largely successful. Traditional Theravada Buddhism remains the dominant religion in Sri Lanka, Myanmar, and Thailand today.

The rise of communist regimes in Laos and Cambodia after 1975 meant disaster for Buddhism there. In Laos, the government curtailed the activities of the Sangha but did not carry out active persecution of the religion. The Khmer Rouge in Cambodia, however, tried to stamp out the religion entirely. They slaughtered monks and nuns and destroyed the Sangha. Of probably 65,000 monks, Cambodia lost all but about 3,000—a whole generation of its most highly educated people. The number of monks is now around 50,000. However, the people who would have passed on the traditions of the faith and learning are gone. Religious training has suffered as a result. Today Cambodia struggles to regain its religious footing.

Buddhism in Modern Asia

By the time of the arrival of the Europeans, the influence of Mahayana Buddhism had already declined in China and Korea. Many Koreans adopted Christianity. In China, Buddhism survived until the coming of the communists, who discouraged all religious practice. During the Cultural Revolution (1966–1976), young Red Guards actively persecuted monks and nuns. Today Chinese monastic Buddhism survives mainly in Taiwan, which has a vigorous Sangha. However, it is estimated that more than 100 million mainland Chinese still practice Buddhism in secret.

Vietnam, colonized by the French, developed a strong minority of Roman Catholics. In North Vietnam, all religion suffered under the communists, but Buddhism remained entrenched in the culture. With reunification in Vietnam, Buddhism has experienced a revival. Today it is estimated that 70 percent of Vietnamese are Buddhist.

In the early seventeenth century, the Japanese became alarmed at what they considered foreign tampering with Japanese affairs. Japan expelled the Christian missionaries and closed its ports to almost all foreigners. Soon afterwards, all Japanese were forbidden to leave Japan. The country was effectively shut off from the world for the next two hundred years. In the mid-nineteenth century, Japan reopened its ports and embraced Western technology. It soon developed into a world power. Although Japan's official religion was Shinto, its various forms of Mahayana Buddhism continued to thrive as a vital force in the life of its people.

Since the end of World War II, the Japanese Sangha has worked to draw lay people into active participation in the religion. Young people's groups, public lectures and discussion classes, and social gatherings are part of the Japanese Buddhist revival. Though newer forms of Buddhism have attracted many followers, the ancient sects still thrive. Japanese Buddhists have played an active part in spreading different forms of Buddhism to Europe and to the United States.

The Tragedy of Tibet

For centuries, Buddhist monks ruled the country of Tibet. The overall ruler of both Tibet's religious life and its government was the Dalai Lama. Tibetans believed him to be a reincarnation of the Buddha himself. In 1949 China invaded Tibet. Two years later China annexed the smaller country. It divided Tibet roughly in half, making half into Chinese provinces.

The current Dalai Lama, born in 1935, is the fourteenth in a line that stretches back more than 640 years. Buddhist priests selected him to be their next leader when he was two years old.

The Dalai Lama, one of the world's best-known and most revered religious figures, has lived in exile for more than forty years.

They raised and educated him. In 1950, at the age of fifteen, he became the ruler of Tibet.

For nine years, the young ruler tried to negotiate with the Chinese. The Chinese, for their part, said they were freeing the Tibetan people from the harsh rule of the Buddhist monks. In 1959, around the city of Lhasa, people rose up against the Chinese. In putting down the uprising, Chinese troops killed as many as 87,000 Tibetan citizens. The Dalai Lama, then twenty-four years old, fled across the Himalaya Mountains to Dharamsala, India. He has lived there in exile ever since.

In the early years of the Chinese occupation, more than 1.2 million Tibetans died. The Chinese destroyed more than 6,200 monasteries. They imprisoned monks and nuns. They took the Buddhist treasures—jewels, gold, silver, statues, and holy items—back to China and sold them. They burned sacred texts.

Tibetans have continued to resist Chinese rule. After anti-Chinese riots in 1989, the Chinese imposed a year of martial law. Throughout the 1990s, they conducted campaigns to persuade Tibetans to abandon their attachment to Buddhism and the Dalai Lama. They searched private homes for religious objects and banned government workers from sending their children to Buddhist schools. In Tibet it is against the law for anyone to have a Buddhist shrine or to own a photograph of the Dalai Lama.

In 1995, the Dalai Lama chose a six-year-old boy to be the next Panchen Lama, the second highest religious figure in Tibetan Buddhism. He will one day be the fifteenth Dalai Lama. The Chinese rejected the Dalai Lama's choice and installed another boy instead. By interfering in the selection of the Panchen Lama, they hope to control the future of Tibetan religion.

In 1999, the fifteen-year-old boy whom the Dalai Lama had chosen as Karmapa, another high-ranking religious figure, escaped from Tibet. The Chinese had previously accepted this young man. As part of their attempt to bring Tibetan religion under their control, they had tried to influence his education, but he rebelled and fled. The next year, Chinese authorities forced more than 800 monks and nuns to leave their monasteries. In all, more than 12,000 monks and nuns have been forced out or imprisoned since the Chinese takeover. About 73 percent of the known political prisoners in Tibet are monks and nuns.

The Dalai Lama maintains a government-in-exile in Dharamsala, India. India permits him and his followers to govern themselves as long as they abide by India's laws. In 1989 the Dalai Lama won the Nobel Peace Prize for his nonviolent efforts to free his country. He has traveled around the world, visiting with world religious and political leaders. Changes in the international scene, particularly the breakup of the Soviet Union, have given him and his followers hope that, one day, Tibet will again be free and its people will be able to worship as they choose.

Buddhism Returns to Mongolia

For Buddhists, one of the most exciting events of the 1990s has been the revival of Buddhism in Mongolia. Mongolians had practiced Buddhism since the sixteenth century. When the communists came into power, they banned all practice of religion. During the 1930s, more than 20,000 monks were executed and 800 monasteries destroyed. A few surviving monks kept the religion alive by meeting in secret.

In 1990 full religious freedom returned to Mongolia. Monks and nuns, now elderly, returned to the temples that were left. In the capital, Ulan Bator, the Gandan monastery had been turned into a museum. It is now a temple again, filled with lay people

■ *Sunrise at the entrance to a Buddhist monastery in Mongolia.*

as well as chanting monks and nuns. Monasteries originally built in the sixteenth and eighteenth centuries are now being restored. The Mongolian government is helping to provide funds, along with outside agencies such as the United Nations.

There has also been a dramatic increase in the number of Mongolian young people who are becoming monks and nuns. Buddhist schools teach philosophy, logic, and language, as well as the music and dance that will be used in Buddhist ceremonies. Mongolian Buddhist art and sculpture are also being revived, using classic materials and techniques.

Buddhism Moves West

In the nineteenth century, British, German, and French scholars began to translate some of the Buddhist scriptures into European languages. Some Europeans found in them new wisdom and a new perspective. During the twentieth century, Buddhism was established in most of Western Europe. It became a presence not only in France, Germany, and the United Kingdom, but also in Austria, Switzerland, the Netherlands, Belgium, Italy, Hungary, Poland, Scandinavia, Spain, and Greece.

In Eastern Europe, Tibetan Buddhism had come to Russia from Mongolia in the seventeenth century. It had been an officially recognized religion there since the 1700s. With the rise of communism, the religion fell on hard times. Monasteries were destroyed or turned into public buildings. Today Buddhism is once again on the rise in the former Soviet Union. The ruined monasteries are being restored, and new ones are being built.

Buddhism Comes to America

In the mid-1800s, a group of New England writers became interested in the thought and philosophy of Asia. They believed that there was an aspect of reality that transcended, or rose above, everyday life, and so they were called Transcendentalists. One of the group was Henry David Thoreau, who wrote *Walden*. This book describes years he spent living in a one-room cabin on the banks of a Massachusetts pond and observing nature. Thoreau, like many of the Transcendentalists, studied Asian thought and belief. He translated the Lotus Sutra from a French version into English. Although Thoreau never embraced Buddhism directly, Buddhists consider *Walden* to be the first American Buddhist sutra.

Meanwhile, Buddhism was entering the United States on the West Coast. The California gold rush of 1849 attracted Chinese prospectors from across the Pacific Ocean. A few years later laborers from China helped to build the transcontinental railroad. Chinese immigrants tended to live together in communities called Chinatowns, where they built Buddhist temples. Most of these early immigrants were members of the Pure Land sect, which had developed in China.

Soon after, the first Japanese contract workers came to work on the plantations of Hawaii after the islands had been annexed by the United States. These immigrants were also primarily of the Pure Land branch of Buddhism. The Pure Land tradition continued, and it is today part of the Buddhist Churches of America and Canada. In Hawaii, it was the beginning of a tradition that would make Buddhism the majority religion of our fiftieth state.

Buddhism in the American Heartland

In 1893, Buddhism came to the American heartland. Chicago hosted the Columbian Exposition that celebrated the progress of science and technology in the United States. The organizers decided to recognize the spiritual side of humanity as well and organized a World Parliament of Religions. Among the Buddhists who attended were Anagarike Dharmapala and a Zen master named Soyen Shaku.

At the parliament, Soyen Shaku met a religious publisher who was looking for a translator. The Zen master recommended a young student who had some knowledge of English. The student was Suzuki Daitsetsu Teitaro, who would become better known as D. T. Suzuki (1870–1966) and would popularize Zen in the United States so that it became a household word.

The young Suzuki made arrangements to go to Illinois. In his last meditation session in Kamakura, he managed (in his words) to "break through"—meaning that he had achieved a higher degree of insight. He was spiritually prepared for his work in the United States. His work had a great influence. He spent eleven years translating Buddhist texts and Japanese commentaries that attracted a wide readership. Later, in the 1950s, he returned to the United States to teach at Columbia University and other schools. His lectures on Buddhism in general and Zen in particular attracted enthusiastic audiences. Millions read his books, such as *Introduction to Zen Buddhism, Living by Zen,* and *The Essentials of Zen Buddhism.*

The Appeal of Zen Buddhism

Why was Zen Buddhism so appealing to Americans? Perhaps for the same reason that it had been in Asia: It put forth the message that people should make the most out of their existence through self-discipline, meditation, and instruction and thus find fulfillment in life. Zen teaches one to live in the present, a view that many Americans share. For the Zen Buddhist, the quality of experience here and now assumes paramount importance. Zen enlightenment consists of the discovery of the profound meaning of day-to-day experience. This was a way of life that could be accepted even while keeping one's own religion.

Zen entered American literature through the writings of the "beat" authors of the 1950s, especially Jack Kerouac and Allen Ginsberg. Today, Zen meditation centers are found throughout the United States. Zen Buddhism claims more than nine million adherents worldwide.

Nichiren Shoshu of America

Nichiren, a branch of Buddhism in the Mahayana tradition, traces its origins to a thirteenth-century Japanese monk named Nichiren (1222–1282). Nichiren taught that the highest truth lay in the Lotus Sutra. He proclaimed that chanting of Namu-myoho-renge-kyo ("Homage be paid to the Lotus Sutra of the Wonderful Dharma") would, by itself, raise consciousness to the level of enlightenment.

Devotion to the Lotus Sutra and commitment to personal improvement are required of all members of Nichiren. Nichiren teaches the importance of overcoming problems in everyday life and asks each person to take responsibility for developing his or her unique potential. Just as people have often created their predicament, so they have the power to cure it through developing "Buddha qualities" such as wisdom and life forces. Buddhism teaches that these qualities are within each of us. The followers of Nichiren believe that as they extend their own wisdom, compassion, and life force, they will gradually extend into a wider sphere of existence.

Soka Gakkai

Over the centuries, the Nichiren sect gained a sizable following in Japan. In 1930, Nichiren leaders formed the Soka Gakkai ("Society for Value Creation") to spread devotion to the Lotus Sutra. After World War II, the organization sent missions to Europe and to North and South America. In the decades since the 1960s it has spread rapidly to the United States.

Soka Gakkai and its international body, Soka Gakkai International, focus on promoting world peace through international cultural exchange. They adhere to the teachings of Nichiren but are far more activist than their parent organization, Nichiren Shoshu. During the 1980s, the two organizations differed sharply on how funds should be allocated. Nichiren leaders felt that Soka Gakkai, with its social projects, was draining

■ *American Buddhists in San Francisco enjoy a discussion at a Soka Gakkai International-USA meeting.*

money away from the parent organization, and particularly from the priesthood. The differences finally led to a rupture between the two groups in 1991, when the head of Nichiren Shoshu excommunicated Soka Gakkai.

In the United States, Soka Gakkai has tried to adapt to American culture. The result is a highly diverse membership. About half of its members are white, eighteen percent African-American, eleven percent Asian and Pacific Islander, seven percent Hispanic/Latino, and the rest "other." Soka Gakkai is thus more diverse than the American population itself, and significantly more diverse than most other religions. Soka Gakkai celebrates this diversity, which it attributes to the value the group places on the worth of the individual regardless of race or culture. Its focus on present-day problems such as the environment, women's issues, and world peace also appeal to many. With about nine million adherents worldwide and perhaps 300,000 in the United States, Soka Gakkai is one of the fastest growing Buddhist organizations.

American Buddhism in the Twentieth Century

Today, estimates of how many people in America are Buddhists vary greatly. There are, however, as many different kinds of Buddhism in the United States as there are in Asia. In the past century, immigrants from all over Asia have brought all of the different Buddhist schools to America. These include Zen and Nichiren from Japan, Vajrayana from Tibet, Ch'an from China, and forms of Theravada from Southeast Asia.

As of now, a division remains between American-born Buddhists and their Asian-born counterparts. Both practice forms of the same religion, but from widely differing cultural perspectives. American Buddhists tend to focus on meditation and its techniques. Lay people, particularly women, play an important role. The Asian Buddhist experience, rooted in hundreds or thousands of years of tradition and culture, is more conservative. Moreover, American Buddhism has been slow to develop a monastic tradition, the mainstay of much Asian Buddhism. For the most part, the two groups do not mix, yet they recognize one another's devotion to the same path.

Buddhism and the Future

In 1950, the World Fellowship of Buddhists was organized to foster fellowship among the many different schools of Buddhism and to spread the faith. Today, the WFB has 140 regional centers in more than 40 countries, serving most of the world's 350 million Buddhists. In the year 2000, it celebrated its fiftieth anniversary by opening the World Buddhist University, a university without walls, in Bangkok, Thailand. This school offers education and training in different parts of the world through a network of Buddhist institutions and scholars.

The World Fellowship of Buddhists works to increase awareness of Buddhism. In 1999, the United Nations formally recognized the day celebrated throughout the Buddhist world as the anniversary of the birth, enlightenment, and Parinirvana of the Buddha, thus realizing one of the WFB's important goals.

Buddhism offers many benefits for the modern world. Modern interpretations of the Buddha's life and teaching have underscored his humanity and his rational approach to the problems of human suffering. Many Buddhist scholars have stressed the relevance of Buddhist teachings to present-day social and ethical issues. The Buddhist teaching of a kinship of all living things is particularly appealing in a world faced with environmental problems. Buddhists claim that their religion can be the basis for a truly democratic society and even for world peace.

The Buddhist emphasis on compassion and wisdom provides high ideals for any society. Whether one leads a religious or a nonreligious life, the teachings of the Buddha make one think and encourage a life of concern for others.

In his Nobel Prize acceptance speech at Oslo, Norway, the Dalai Lama quoted a traditional prayer. It summarizes the high ideals of Buddhism:

"For as long as space endures,
And for as long as living beings remain,
Until then may I, too, abide
To dispel the misery of the world."

GLOSSARY

Alms—In Buddhism, the offering of food to monks on their daily rounds and the donation of goods and money to the monasteries.

Arhat—A Buddhist monk who is free from all illusions and who has achieved personal enlightenment.

Ahimsa—The noninjury of living beings.

Amitabha—The Bodhisattva whose name means "Buddha of Boundless Light" and who dwells in the paradise called the Pure Land.

Avalokitesvara—The Bodhisattva who looks on his devotees with compassion and love. The most popular Bodhisattva.

Bardo—A human soul between the stages of after-death and rebirth.

Bardo Thodol—The Tibetan name for the Book of the Dead.

Bikkhu or **Bikshu**—A fully ordained monk who has left his home and renounced all his possessions in order to follow the Way of the Buddha.

Bodhisattva—A being in the final stages of attaining Buddhahood, who has vowed to help all sentient beings achieve Nirvana, or enlightenment, before he himself achieves it.

Bodhi Tree or **Bo Tree**—The tree beneath which the meditating Gautama sat before he achieved enlightenment.

Bodhidharma—The legendary monk who brought Buddhism from India to China in the sixth century C.E.

Buddha—The "Enlightened One."

Buddha-nature—The nature innate in every sentient being. The potential for attaining Buddhahood.

Butsu-dan—Japanese Buddhist household altar.

Chaitya—An assembly hall for monks.

Dharma—The ultimate law, or doctrine, as taught by Buddha, which consists of the Four Noble Truths and the Eightfold Path.

Dhyana—A state of mind achieved through higher meditation.

Dukkha—Suffering, emptiness, impermanence.

Hinayana—Literally, "small vehicle." A term used by the Mahayanists to describe earlier orthodox sects of Buddhism (Theravada School). Their scriptures are written in Pali, an ancient Indian language. *see also* **Theravada.**

Karma—Literally, "deed." A concept that binds its followers to an endless cycle of birth, death, and rebirth and, according to one's deeds in life, determines the condition of one's rebirth.

Koan—A riddle, tale, or short statement used by Zen masters to bring their students to sudden insight.

Lama—Literally, "superior one." A Buddhist monk of Tibet.

Mahayana—Literally, "great vehicle." One of the two major forms of Buddhism, Mahayana is considered the more liberal and practical. Its scriptures are written in Sanskrit. *see also* **Theravada.**

Maitreya—Literally, "Friendly One." The Bodhisattva who embodies the virtues of compassion and benevolence.

Manjushri—Literally, "Beautiful Auspicious One." The Bodhisattva who embodies the virtues of wisdom and eloquence.

Mantra—Ritual sound, word, or phrase used to evoke a certain religious effect.

Mara—The personification of evil. The god of death.

Nirvana—Literally, "extinction." The ultimate goal of Buddhists, characterized as the extinction of both craving and the separate "ego." The state of peace and quietude attained by extinguishing all illusions.

Parinirvana—Death of the Buddha.

Samsara—The continuous cycle of birth, death, and rebirth.

Sangha—An organized assembly of Buddhist monks.

Stupa—A dome, or pagoda, in which sacred relics are deposited.

Sutta or **Sutra**—Literally, "thread" or "string." A scripture containing the teachings of Buddha.

Theravada—Literally, "School of the Elders." Also known as Hinayana. One of the two major forms of Buddhism, Theravada is considered to be the original and orthodox form of Buddhism. *see also* **Hinayana.**

Tipitaka or **Tripitaka**—Literally, "Three Baskets." According to Buddhist belief, the scriptures were stored in three baskets, dividing Buddha's teachings into the code of discipline for monks, his sermons and discourses, and the higher doctrine (Buddhist philosophy and psychology).

Urna—A mark on the Buddha's forehead, between his eyebrows, that signifies his great intuition.

Ushanisha—A protuberance atop Buddha's head that signifies his great wisdom.

Vihara—Cave dwellings for the monks.

Zen or **Ch'an**—Forms of Mahayana Buddhism in Japan and China, respectively.

FOR FURTHER READING

Bishop, Peter, and Michael Darnton, eds. *The Encyclopedia of World Faiths*. New York: Facts On File, 1988.

Conze, Edward, ed. *Buddhist Scriptures*. London: Penguin Books, 1959.

Dalai Lama. *The Compassionate Life*. Boston: Wisdom Publications, 2001.

____. *Freedom in Exile*. New York: Harper Perennial, 1990.

____. *An Open Heart*. Boston: Little, Brown and Company, 2001.

Fontana, David. *Discover Zen*. San Francisco: Chronicle Books, 2001.

Hagen, Steve. *Buddhism Plain and Simple*. Boston: Broadway Books, 1997.

Ikeda, Daisaku. *The Way of Youth*. Santa Monica, Calif.: Middleway Press, 2000.

Murcott, Susan. *The First Buddhist Women*. Berkeley, Calif.: Parallax Press, 1991.

Parrinder, Geoffrey, ed. *World Religions from Ancient History to the Present*. New York: Facts On File, 1984.

Saddhatissa, Hammalawa. *Before He Was Buddha: The Life of Siddhartha*. Berkeley, Calif.: Seastone, 1998, 2000.

Smith, Jean. *The Beginner's Guide to Zen Buddhism*. New York: Belltower, 2000.

Smith, Huston. *The Illustrated World Religions*. San Francisco: HarperSanFrancisco, 1994.

Suzuki, D. T. *An Introduction to Zen Buddhism*. New York: Grove Press, 1964.

INDEX